Shhh...I've Got a Secret

Kelley Alsobrook

What people are saying about "Shhh...I've Got a Secret"

Pastor Matt Anzivino/ Lead Pastor - The House Memphis:

It is with a profound sense of gratitude coupled with a sincere feeling of urgency that I recommend this book to you, the reader. Gratitude, because I have the privilege of encouraging you to read this book which tells the life-story of a modern day hero. Kelley is a women of God who had every right to become a victim of her past. Instead, she chose to redeem her past by becoming a voice of victory, hope and love. The feeling of urgency comes because of the millions of people who are, as we speak, caught in the web of the tragic epidemic of this generation, sex trafficking. Kelley is one of those who has been set free by the Grace of God. Her story, and this book, represent the voice of those who desperately need our help. It is my prayer that after reading Kelley's story, you will be motivated to become a part of a growing army of people who refuse to stand idle. We must, now more than ever, stand for those who cannot stand for themselves and defend the defenseless. Let's do everything in our power to see the captives of SEX TRAFFICKING set free!

Hope Manasseh/Ritual abuse Survivor

"Shhh...I've Got a Secret" is a powerful and inspiring example of the freedom that is possible when the human heart finds our will despite overwhelming obstacles and presses forward for what can be, irrespective of what has been. Kelley held nothing back in creating a roadmap, based NOT on her journey or life story but instead in the unchanging and unfailing nature of God.

Dare to step into the journey and if refuse to give up, settle or stay hidden in the secrets that Jesus already knows you will rise above the shame just like Kelley is doing every day.

Michaela Floyd/Human Trafficking Survivor:

In "Shhh...I've Got a Secret" Kelley unflinchingly and boldly takes the reader by the hand and allows them to walk with her through unbearable childhood pain, excruciating abuse and exploitation as a young adult and finally the raw and faltering faith journey toward a God who showed her all the beauty and purpose he had bestowed within her from the beginning. You will cry, laugh and sometimes shake your head, but in the end Kelley lays it out lesson by lesson how you too can see yourself through the eyes of a loving God who created each of us for a divine purpose. This book should be read by every woman in jail or in recovery, or anyone struggling to see past their own pain and trauma to understand how to go on or where to turn.

Ms. Pineapple Soda/Childhood Abuse Survivor:

"As the old saying goes, "You couldn't walk a mile in my shoes". Through Kelley's tell all, you'll quickly agree that fact still stands! Her story educates, brings forth awareness, and earns a great level of respect for her power within to succeed, console, and heal."

Wendie Snow/Domestic Violence Survivor:

Amazing, empowering, inspiring, jaw dropping, emotional best seller of a book. Also, a wakeup call for victims of any adversity. For someone like me, it is an awakening, a tear jerker, a slap in the face, a realization of not wanting to give up. To get back up and fight and be a survivor not a victim. Release it all and regain your freedom, independence, and self-worth.

Lilly K./Ritual abuse & human trafficking survivor

Kelley has demonstrated a courage not her own. In this powerful book, Kelley faces the brutality of being trafficked. She has arisen out of the ashes of human trafficking and domestic violence into a whole new life. Kelley has shown that anyone can escape brutality and find healing. She has a beautiful soul and has demonstrated a passion and a fire to help other survivors no matter who they are. If you want a powerful story that will make you see the effects of trafficking and understand the necessity of fighting trafficking this is the book.

Dedication

This book is dedicated to all that have been broken, beaten, battered and forgotten. Also, to the women (you know who you are) that I have had the privilege of sharing with and counseling. I walk with you through the journey of healing, and together we are mending our wounded hearts. Always remember, you are exceptional, you are strong, and you are worthy of so much more! It is time to release all secrets, heal, and rise up! Please know that your adversity does not define you, that you are loved, and that you are ENOUGH!

Disclaimer

Some names have been changed in order to protect myself as well as for privacy reasons.

Table of Contents

Published by CreateSpace Independent Publishing Platform

ISBN: 978-0-9853795-9-9

Disclaimer: The events are portrayed to the best of Kelley Alsobrooks memory. While all the stories in this book are true, some names and identifying details have been changed to protect the privacy of the people involved. This book contains some graphic language and explicit scenes. It is not recommended for a younger reader.

Back cover photograph by Lauren Trantham

Cover design by Pineapple Soda

Print interior design and eBook formatting by Jeffrey Harris

Edited by Hope Manasseh

Introduction

Last fall Kelley sent me a text asking if we could talk. I knew from the tone of the text she had something pressing to discuss. "Hope, I have a big favor to ask you" were her words as she answered my call. Kelley tends to approach asking for help almost solemnly. I understand this and tend to do the same. When you have lived far more of your life believing you don't deserve help or if for some reason asking has validity that your request is always an excessive burden asking becomes a solemn and risky endeavor.

"Do you remember that memoir I deleted?"

Hmm... you mean the one I didn't delete - yes of course I do Kelley!"

"You kept that - it was terrible?"

"Yeah it was a pretty rough draft but that does not mean you or your story suck It just means you need to work through some details before you decide if you want to write."

"Interesting you should say that, because that is what I wanted to talk about. Hope, I have felt God pressing me to write for a while, but I am not a writer. I don't know how to write. That draft was so bad and so hard." Do you remember that presentation I gave last weekend?

"Yes"

"Hope, I found my passion and, no one is talking about it." I don't want to write a memoir, and really nobody wants to read it! There are enough survivor accounts. The world will not notice one more or one less survivor story. Hope I want to help women work through the shame. Nobody is talking about that and so many of us are stuck drowning in shame. Woman today are killing ourselves carrying shame like some badge of honor."

"I wish you could have been there this weekend. I have been trying to figure out why I am in this space for months. This weekend I answered that question. I want to help start conversations about the secrets that keep us trapped and hiding."

"Will you help me?"

Kelley, you know I love talking about secrets and hard topics, but what are you asking me to do…

I don't remember how long it took Kelley to get her feet and head back on the planet but I remember the tone in her voice as she finished sharing her vision and asked me to write this introduction. She was right about three things…

1.   Her first draft / outline of a memoir was terrible!

2.   The world definitely does not need another survivor story.

3.   Women need help and understanding to step out of our shame AND Kelley has a gift for making it okay to break out of taboo and painful secrets.

Tomorrow the manuscript will be uploaded to being the final formatting and processing for self-publication. In the months between that first call and tonight I have watched and walked with Kelley through some deeply personal and painful places. Each place was a choice as she pushed herself to walk out and press through the same processes she shares within these pages.

You may not be able to see the tear stains that were poured out, over these pages, but I know them well. It's an honor to write this introduction as a testimony to the woman I walked with as she was stretch, often past the place of breaking. These are not mere words or inspirational stories thrown together to convince you. Every detail was carefully chosen to demonstrate that even our most painful moments, when exposed to truth represent **not** defeat, BUT instead life opportunities for growth and understanding. Healing happens as we step into, instead of deny, minimize or excuse our wounds and hidden shame. We are created, hardwired if you will, to step head on into our shame, our past, our fears, and our failures. It is in these defining moments that cause us to grow, heal and find our purpose. Even more as we step into, on our way through, life's struggles and uncomfortable times our pain, shame, disappointments and failures come face to face with our potential.

Potential that cannot be hidden or choked out by shame or our pain. Freedom comes not in an instant but moment by moment as we just hold on and take another step head on into shame, pain, disappointment, fear, failure and our secrets. Healing is not easy, but it will be the most worthwhile journey you take.

"Shhh...I've Got a Secret" is a powerful and inspiring example of the freedom that is possible when the human heart finds our will despite overwhelming obstacles and presses forward for what can be, irrespective of what has been. Kelley held nothing back in creating a roadmap, based NOT on her journey or life story but instead in the unchanging and unfailing nature of God.

Dare to step into the journey and if refuse to give up, settle or stay hidden in the secrets that Jesus already knows you will rise above the shame just like Kelley is doing every day.

Peace in Christ,

Hope Manasseh

Acknowledgements

First and foremost, I want to thank God for giving me the strength and the courage to write this book. Without God I can do nothing.

I want to thank Hope Manasseh for not only her countless hours of editing but for all the time she has spent counseling me through this process. She has been there when I was ready to give up, when I got angry, cried and felt all of the emotions of reliving the past. Hope, you have truly been my rock when I thought I wouldn't make it and for that I am forever grateful.

To Rebecca Bender and Kathy Bryan, through the Elevate class you showed me how much potential I really did have and gave me the courage to actually live out my dreams and not just dream about them and I thank you from the bottom of my heart.

Ms. Pineapple Soda, you did an amazing job on my book cover and made sure everything was perfect. Thank you so much for your love and support through this process. I know this hasn't been an easy project but you helped make it happen!!

Jeff Harris, thank you so much for taking the time out of your very busy schedule in order to make sure my book was formatted correctly. It was a challenge but you really did an amazing job. I cant thank you enough.

Donna Black, Ha Tran & Karen Hurst, you guided me through the beginning stages of this process and would not let me give up. You wanted me to succeed so you didn't sugar coat anything, you told me what I needed to hear and have continued to be my cheerleaders throughout the process and helped with resources that I would have otherwise struggled to get. Thank you so much for your honesty and friendship.

To my "Warrior Goddesses" …I love each & every one of you so much. You have loved me and supported me and I am forever grateful! Each and every one of you are very special to me! Never forget how amazing you truly are!

Pastor Matt & Shannon, thank you for your love, friendship and leadership. You never gave up on me and have been by my side as I continue to heal and grow in God. I love you deeply.

To so many friends along the way of my healing process that loved me even when there were days that I was so unlovable, thank you for standing by my side!

To all of my "survivor/warrior" sisters (and brothers) I love y'all so very much. We have a bond that nobody could ever understand. I am so grateful to each and every one of you that have allowed me into your lives. We are knit together in such a unique way and I wouldn't trade any of you for anything in the world.

To my incredible husband, Keefe. Your love helps me get through all my good, bad and ugly days. I thank you for all of your love & support. I love you more than words can ever express. You are truly a gift from GOD that I will never take for granted. You are MY Boaz!

PART 1

MY SECRETS

A Trauma Filled Childhood

A life doomed before it even started!!! I was doomed before my entrance and first hello into this world. My daddy dearest telling me a horrific story... when my mother was pregnant with me for unknown reason to me she tried jumping off a high dresser in order to terminate her pregnancy. **To kill me, her unborn child**. This moment evoked a memory. As a child to hear those words they penetrated into my heart. My heart was broken into millions of pieces. Why? What had I done to her? Was it a difficult pregnancy? Was she concerned that by giving life to me she would have to give up hers? Or was she terrified of her husband...and thought that it was better that I didn't exist? Why? Why didn't my mother want to give birth to me? Those questions go unanswered. At the young tender age of 11 or 12 I went to bed and cried myself to sleep ...I believed him. I was thinking that maybe I was better off if I were never born. If my parents could not love me than who could. I began my journey of a love less, worthless child. Feeling like a worthless piece of garbage.

I remember while my mom and dad were still together my mom was terrified of my dad. She was a subservient to him. She had no say about anything. No decisions, no control.

One day for the very first time I saw her take control she had put her foot down when my dad beat my sister when she was 7 or 8 (not his biological daughter) and she screamed at him to never touch her again. And he never did, even after my mom left him when I was 10 and my sister chose to stay with him instead of going with my mom and me.

I think one of the ways that I dealt with the turmoil in my family was food. In the middle of the night I would sneak into the kitchen and get something to eat but that was put to an end when they put a buzzer on my door. Can you imagine, at 8 or 9 years old having a buzzer on my door so they knew if I was leaving my room? It was a prison, not a home. I felt like I had no freedom to be a child.

I learned early on that you could pay for friendships. I was always picked on in elementary school because I was chunky and I just wanted to fit in with the other kids so I stole an old set of checks from my mother and would write checks to the school store to buy color paper, cool pencils, book covers and anything else that I thought the kids would like just so they would like me and be my friend. I did get caught however after the 3rd or 4th time doing this because I was writing the checks in crayon! How I got away with it the first few times is beyond me.

When my dad brought it up over dinner I just knew he would flip out but it was actually my mom that was extremely angry. She told my dad to get the belt and go beat the hell out of me. But what my dad did actually surprised me. I was scared to death because his beatings always hurt so bad. But once we got into my room and he closed the door he started hitting the bed with the belt and he told me to act like he was hitting me. He actually thought what I did was funny and thought the ladies that were accepting the checks were kind of dumb. He kept those checks for years and every so often would tease me about it.

My mother had enough of my dad and left him when I was 10. She packed up her Oldsmobile 442 with the birds, our stuff and away we went. We drove from Miami to New Jersey to my grandmother's house. I had always loved going to my grandmother's house whenever we visited because her and my grandfather were so sweet and the atmosphere of their home was loving and not so full of turmoil. My grandfather was absolutely one of the most amazing men that I had ever met. He was so full of love and was one of the only people that truly showed that he loved me. He was very well respected in the town that they lived in.

Now my grandmother on the other hand she loved me but any time I did anything that was considered bad or if I made a mistake she would always ask me, "Why can't you be like your sister? She's always so good she does everything right."

So once again here I was feeling inferior because I wasn't as good as my sister. Now don't get me wrong I love my sister and I looked up to her so much. My sister was seven years older than me and so of course she knew better than I did and was very smart, had already started a good career and was going to college. She was the levelheaded one, the one who never got in trouble, and from the perspective of a ten-year-old deeply hurting and neglected child the favorite child, who did everything right AND she was my hero. I remember the night that, while I was sleeping, my father came into my room and started hitting me. On this night my sister ran in the room jumped up on the bed and told him "No you are not going to touch her leave her alone." She was never scared of my father and I think that was one of the things I admired so much about her. She could stand up to him and he would never say anything to her. After that incident he came into the room and told me that we were going to go to Disney World. And of course being a little kid, desperate for acceptance, I convinced myself that the trip made everything all better. My sister seemed to be my only hope. She was the only person that could ever seem to keep my dad calm. I had always looked up to my sister, she was everything that I wasn't and my family let me know that all the time! Sadly, she couldn't always save me. She was 7 years older than me, working and earning a good living and I was the "pain in the butt" little sister. I know she loved me but she was gone a lot of the time whether for school, her job at the dealership, job on the fishing boat or just hanging out with her friends.

My mother and father had shared custody of me so there were times that I would spend about six months to a year with my mom and then I would spend a year with my dad, so I would go back and forth between the two of them. My mother had significant psychological issues and at times spent time in the hospital for treatment. During those times I was sent to my dad's. He reminded me constantly that I was better off there with him because my mother was so unstable. I felt trapped, indebted and desperate at the same time. I loved the time I got to spend with my mom because life with my mom was like an adventure. She had her moments of anger and yelling and punished me harshly, at times, but I figured that was all pretty normal. When I was with my mom I didn't feel like I had to walk on eggshells and be careful about everything that I did.

I was especially happy when a year or two after leaving my dad my mom met my step dad and they got married. He was very sweet, laid back; loving, caring, and he treated me as if I was his own daughter. He even wanted to adopt me and give me his last name so I could truly be his daughter but my father wasn't having it. For a while we live in a small one-bedroom apartment and it was getting too cramped so I went back to live with my father.

I can still hear those words echoing in my head. "You are nothing and you will never be anything!" I can remember just sitting in my room feeling so alone, the pain from those words cut into my heart so deep. I grew up feeling increasingly worthless, unloved, unwanted and unable to understand what I had done wrong. Why did my father hate me so much? All I ever wanted was my dad to love me and be proud of who me for no other reason than who I was moment by moment. Every child needs the security of knowing they are loved unconditionally by their parent. Instead it was as if I disgusted him.

My room became my sanctuary. I spent most of my time in my room with my imaginary friends, who of course loved me perfectly and no matter what. I had imaginary friends into my early teenage years because I craved love so much. It was my way of getting away from all of the ugly that was outside of my room.

As a kid and even into my teenage years I always felt I was different than the kids I went to school with. I never felt good enough, pretty enough, smart enough or popular enough! I always felt like I was alone and just wanted to fit in and feel like I was loved.

I learned about fear, from my father, as a youngster. He was a very intimidating man to all he met. He was a large man and exuded power and authority. It was in his voice and certainly in the way he looked when he was angry. His leg would shake under the table and He would grit his teeth and the look on his face was as if the devil was looking at me. There were times that the way he yelled at me left me so terrified I peed myself.

My dad would say all the time whatever happens in this house stays in this house. Nobody was to know our business. I was too afraid to tell anyone what I was going through and what I was feeling. I understand now that lots of parents say things like this, which makes life more confusing for an abused or neglected kid, because it reinforces the belief that what is happening at home is normal and must be our fault.

I often have to wonder if my dad didn't have some sort of psychological issues himself. I know that his childhood was pretty horrific. His mother didn't show him the love he needed as a child.

Instead of raising him she would put him in orphanages. While in the orphanage he was abused horribly and sodomized by the other boys. It's no wonder my father turned out the way he did. He had no role model of what it was to be a parent and he lived with some very deep wounds that were never healed.

By the time I reached my teenage years he had my family convinced that I was a liar, and untrustworthy which meant no one believed me when I tried to talk about even minor instances of abuse. As a child life was simply unbearably complicated and confusing. As an adult I can see that all of these things my dad did were put together to keep his abuse and neglect hidden and protect himself at my expense. He would constantly accuse me of things that I never did such as sleeping with the mechanics at his job.

I remember one incident in particular, he came home and was mad about something at work and he hit me so hard that I flipped over the recliner and then he started kicking me with the steel-toed boots he always wore. The pain was so bad that with each kick it felt like my ribs and back was on fire. It felt like the bones were cracking and I just knew this would be the beating that would kill me.

With each kick he screamed insults and lies at me while I curled up and wondered would it ever end. My self-perception came from the hateful vile words my dad screamed at me, including the story about my mom not wanting me, and from my mom's inability to protect me.

After years of being called a whore, a slut, and a screw-up I accepted and believed in my heart every one of his vile, hateful and degrading labels; until the only thing that made sense was to accept what I was.

Life with my dad was terrifying, belittling and hopeless most of the time, but in the midst of hell there were also good times. My favorite times with my dad were on Saturday mornings when he would cook breakfast for us. It was usually just the two of us and it was always a calm and peaceful time. And I have to say, the man could definitely cook! He could take leftovers and make them taste like a gourmet meal.

Another thing my father taught me was about strong work ethics. Since he was parts & service director of a large dealership he would take me to work with him every day off from school and summer vacations. I started working at the age of 12. He made sure I learned everything I could about the auto industry and since I wasn't old enough for the company to pay me he would pay me out of his pocket. We would go to dinner every Friday night and when I would get up and use the restroom I would come back to find money under my placemat. He tried to teach me about saving money but I wasn't very good at that. I was making money and I wanted to spend it.

Like every other part of life with my dad the big downfall to working with him was his violent, unpredictable temper. If I didn't do something right he would call me into his office and scream, at me, at the top of his lungs.

It wasn't unusual for him to throw a cup of coffee at me, as he went into his rage. I was so embarrassed because the other employees would see this going on and do nothing, leaving me feeling so ashamed. I guess I believed that my existence and constant screw-up's were the problem. I could not, at that point in my life, fathom that the problem was my dad.

My 8th grade year was a huge turning point in my life. My relationship with my dad started to change. My sister was going to night school so it was just he and I at home. It started out where he wanted me to get closer to him at the kitchen table; it was uncomfortable to me at first because this seemed so awkward. The closeness was odd to me because he wanted me to sit on his lap and it was not normal. He then started inviting me into his room to watch a movie with him. The type of movies he wanted me to watch with him were not movies that any adult would watch with a child. They were very graphic in nature and I saw things that I never saw before. I got my first impression of a man and a woman together through those movies. The frequency started to continue, every time my sister would leave for school. I was truly uncomfortable and at the same time I had always just wanted my dad to love me. In my child like mind I thought that this was how fathers showed love to their daughters. While watching these movies he would have me lay close to him in the bed and at times he would touch me the way these people in the movies would touch each other. It graduated to far more than touching and although uncomfortable and in the depths of my mind I knew this was wrong but I felt like for the first time that I mattered to him. The molestation increased in frequency and intensity. My dad became bolder and bolder in his molestation as time went on, until I wasn't the only person that he molested. I learned to have only a few friends and rather than them invite them to my house I chose to go to their house in order to keep them safe. The strategy also provided me with an me to escape from what was happening at home. My older sister had no clue about what happened every night, when she left for work or school. By the time she got home I learned to be asleep so that she would not see my tears. There were so many ways that I silently screamed for help. I didn't know how to share this with anyone else. I was too ashamed and embarrassed and knew that nobody would believe me because my father had already planted the seed that I was a liar.

I would run away, my grades dropped and that was so unlike me. I actually failed school that year. But even that went unquestioned. There was clearly something going on with me, I had always been a good student, but no one in my life asked or made any effort to find out what had caused the major changes in me. It was as if I went unnoticed and was invisible. I felt like nobody cared enough to see my pain. I can tell you that while I understand many people say and do nothing because they don't want to be wrong, I also know that kids don't go through major shifts in their personality, habits, friend groups, or grades without a big reason, it would be much better to pay attention and ask questions to figure out what changed and help the child through that and not worry about being wrong. Not every child who has major changes is being molested, but for sure every child needs safe caring adults to help navigate whatever the changes are. The "affection" my dad was showing to me ended when he found the love of his life. He had set his attentions to someone new. Once again I became insignificant and was so confused, because I knew in my heart that stuff should not have happened but at the same time I needed my dad to want and care about me.

When I turned 16 my dad told me that I should quit school, get my GED and go to college. His reasoning behind that was that I would gain more experience in the world than I would in school. So I quit school and started taking GED classes at night and worked at the dealership during the day.

I started getting into trouble and doing really stupid things like stealing money, renting cars without even having a driver's license, running away from home, becoming promiscuous and as I look back it was all for attention. I was missing that love and affection that I wanted so badly but didn't feel I was getting from home. I was acting out and just didn't care anymore whether I lived or died. I didn't feel like anybody else cared so why should I? My suicide plan was complete when I found out I was pregnant with my oldest daughter, Davianna. Despite all the life I had experienced, I was so naïve that I didn't realize I was pregnant until well into my seventh month. I had been madly in love with her father for what felt like a life time. We had been intimate only once when I got pregnant. I didn't know how to tell him, so I opted to say nothing. I guess I hoped that somehow, the fairytale life every little girl dreams of would somehow just happen.

Her father came to see me after I came home from the hospital and he knew right away that she was his daughter! My jaw fell open so hard I left a dent on the floor, when He told me that he wanted to raise her together. He was a small time "dope boy". When my dad found out, that we wanted to raise her together, he told me that if I continued to be with him he would have him arrested for statutory rape. My dad was no joke when it came to his image and I knew he would follow through. I was terrified that the man I was madly in love with would be arrested, so I left him. He then married someone else; leaving me heartbroken and alone with a baby! I was determined to be a good and responsible parent. I got a job, I paid for things my daughter needed and even paid "rent" to stay at my dad's house. I felt that since I was 18 I should be able to do as I pleased but my father didn't view me as a capable adult, so I felt I had no choice but to leave.

On My Own

Here I was, eighteen, pretty naïve and now living on my own! With no money saved and nobody to help me, I moved in with a friend until I could get a better job and get my own place. It didn't take me long at all to have a job with a temp agency, my own place and my own car. The fact that I did not have a driver's license was, at the time, a minor detail, from my perspective. I am still proud of how well I did, as an eighteen-year-old, new, inexperienced and wounded mom. I'm especially proud of me, in this period, when I look back with my now grown-up understanding and recognize the limited support and gargantuan challenges me and Davianna faced.

Like many abused teens and women, I seemed to be attracted to the "bad boys". My younger daughter's father was also a "bad boy". My decision making around how I handled telling him that we were going to have a baby didn't get better the second time. I knew Rico for a few years before we started connecting. Rico would spend a few nights with me and then disappear for a few days, which made me crazy insecure and jealous. One night my insecurities talked me into buying a bottle of MD 20/20. Drinking was not a regular habit.

I don't handle alcohol well! When Rico came back we had a heated argument. I was so drunk that I ran out of the apartment and across the street when BAM, I got hit by a car. The car hit me so hard that I flipped in the air from the front of the car to the back and onto the road. I was taken by ambulance to the emergency room where they took all kinds of tests and x-rays. I had no broken bones but was pretty scraped up and banged up and then the doctor dropped a bombshell on me. He said, "By the way, your baby is just fine!" WHAT?!?! I was pregnant??? That was the last thing I expected to hear. My initial reaction was panic because I could barely take care of my oldest daughter. How was I going to take care of another baby? I didn't believe in abortion so I swore I would be the best mom I could!

Due to the accident, I ended up losing my job at the temp agency, which led me to lose my apartment as well. The first couple of nights after I lost my apartment, my daughter and I slept in front of the apartment building in my car. One morning my sister pulled up next to me, clearly seeing we were sleeping in the car and said, "So, what are you doing?" I told her that I had lost my apartment and all she said was, "Oh, Ok." And drove off. I was so hurt and angry that she responded that way. How could she just not care that we are sleeping in the car with nowhere to go?

Rico decided to take me to his uncle's house so we wouldn't be homeless but a couple of weeks later I woke up to his uncle groping me and trying to kiss me. It was so disgusting!! When Rico found out he was so mad that he went crazy on his uncle, cussing him out and it almost got physical. After leaving there we went to a friend of his house but I couldn't stay there long because his friend's wife kept asking me to sleep with her husband because he was obsessed with me. I was angry with Rico because he was with his girlfriend, I was hormonal due to pregnancy and I just couldn't take the pressure anymore of this woman constantly begging me to sleep with her husband so I did and it definitely made my situation so much worse than it already was. They were arguing all the time because she was so insecure and felt like I was a threat, Rico was highly pissed off and wanted nothing to do with me and I found myself homeless and alone again. Just my baby girl and me.

How had my life spun so out of control? Where were we gonna go? I certainly wasn't going back to my father's house. I was extremely stressed which was no good for my pregnancy.

I found a shelter to stay in during my pregnancy. It was for women only and a small facility and very homey. I loved the director but I couldn't emotionally handle being close to her. She was straightforward, by nature; I was emotionally devastated and crippled as a result of a life time of abuse, neglect and disappointment. When she genuinely pointed out my patterns or weakness's, to help me, I reacted by falling apart or exploding because I could not handle her not being happy with me. I needed an abundance of love to fill my empty hurting heart and without that I was just not able to settle in and feel secure enough to handle anything that sounded like criticism. A lot of times I felt like she didn't care when she was getting on to me about my behaviors and my anger but in reality she did care and just wanted me to do better but I couldn't see it at the time.

While living at the shelter I had a job at our local newspaper in the call center. It was pretty stressful but I was determined to work and save money until I had my baby. She wasn't due until January 1st but on November 17th my water broke and the director knew it was time for me to deliver even though I was convinced it was a false alarm.

How could it be time? She still had 6 weeks to go! She was coming so fast that they barely had time to get me into the delivery room. And there she was, another beautiful baby girl. Apparently there were some complications during delivery because the doctors said her hips were out of place and she had to wear a brace on her legs to try to get her hips back in place.

I brought my new baby home to the shelter and about 2 days later Rico shows up to see her. He swore he would be there for her but he never came back. I was so full of anger and depression after having Bryony that I was kicked out of the shelter. I had no clue what I was going to do. Now I had 2 babies and no place to go. I went across the street to the Wendy's and as I was sitting there a woman came up to me handed me what I thought was a piece of paper and said, "God told me to give this to you." As she walked away I looked in my hand and it was a $100 bill. All I could do was cry. I didn't even know who this God was that she was talking about but I took that money and got me and my babies a hotel room for 2 nights.

I had such a struggle with Bryony. It was as if she could feel my stress and would scream if I came anywhere near her. I didn't know what to do. A friend let us stay with her but the more I tried to bond with Bryony the more she screamed and hollered. Anybody could pick her up but me. One night I got so frustrated and angry that I called my sister and screamed out, "Come and get this f***in baby, I can't take her anymore." My sister wanted to get both Davianna and Bryony but I was so attached to Davianna that I couldn't let her go. I held on to so much guilt and shame for feeling the way I handled the situation with Bryony. She hated me from the day I gave birth to her and it hurt me so deep that I lashed out. As I look back now, I probably should have let my sister take Davianna as well because I was such an unfit mother. I had no clue how to raise kids. Heck, I couldn't even take care of myself. There was so much drama, turmoil and depression, in my life, when one of my "friends" introduced me to cocaine. That first high was awesome because I felt I could do anything. When I got high I either had no emotions or believed I could manage my feelings so getting and staying high seemed like a good plan. There was just too much pain, too much loneliness and so much self-hatred that what I really would have wanted was to end it all.

I still wasn't stable. I continued to move from place to place. I found myself getting into situations I had no business getting myself into.

Friends would open their home to my daughter and me but most of these friends were in relationships. I must have had a sign across my forehead that said, "I am broken and desperate! Please take advantage of me" because it always seemed that the boyfriend would approach me in a sexual way. I was so broken and quite frankly so stupid that I really thought they liked me and would leave their wife/girlfriend for me!! Yeah I know, I wasn't much of a friend was I? Needless to say it usually ended up with arguments and getting put out of wherever we happened to be staying.

There was even one incident when I came home to one of the places I was staying at and got jumped by "my friend" and a couple of her friends. I didn't even see it coming. I hadn't done anything this time but she was accusing me of trying to sleep with her man. All I remember from that night was 2 of them pounding me with their fists and she was hitting me with a baseball bat while another one was holding my daughter. All I could think of with each blow was please don't hurt my daughter. As they were beating me they kept screaming how they were going to take my daughter because I was such an unfit mother. That was hurting me deeper than all the blows that my body was enduring. It seemed this beating would never end and I just knew I was going to die that night and my baby would be without her mother. Finally, one of the neighbors, an elderly woman came out and stopped them. She grabbed my daughter and took me to her house so I could get cleaned up. Bloody and bruised up pretty badly I needed to figure out what I was going to do. I had to get my own place and not depend on anyone else. This amazing woman helped me get healed up physically over the next couple of weeks and then it was time to move on.

I started working as a waitress at a restaurant on the beach and decided to move into one of the hotels close to where I was working. I found myself struggling because even though it was a pay by the week hotel, nothing fancy, I had a hard time finding a babysitter at times so I didn't work a whole lot so I wasn't making the money I needed to make in order to keep a roof over our head and that's when I met Romero.

Life of a Prostitute

I lived in a hotel on the beach, when I met a man who seemed to have it all together, a nice car, and nice clothes. He carried himself with quite a bit of confidence. My focus was on finding a man to take care of me and Davianna. I was so excited that I had found "the one" that was going to take care of me and my daughter that I rushed in when he showed interest. I was so wrong! I missed so many red flags, in my desperation and naivety. I honestly believed there was a genuine interest in my daughter and me but that was far from the truth. Looking back, I now understand his interest went no deeper than the money he could make off me.

Romero was so smooth. He seemed to listen intently when I talked about my failures and struggles and it seemed like he cared about my dreams. He told me all the time that everything was going to be ok and he promised to take care of my daughter and me. He was buying us food, paying for our room and he frequently bought toys, clothes and diapers for my daughter. He was my dream come true why would I question his motives? For the first time in a long time I believed that everything was going to be ok. I was so desperate that I saw what I wanted to see. Looking back, I see lots of red flags. Now I know so much more. I'm not that same scared teenager and I finally understand the difference between love and manipulation

One of the big red flags was the woman staying with him in his room but he told me that was his sister and being so naïve I believed him.

After a couple of weeks of "wooing" me Romero told me that I needed to help with making money. I told him I would get a job and he said he already had a job for me. I asked him what it was and that's when he said I was gonna turn tricks for him. He was so nonchalant about it. I just sat there in disbelief! I couldn't do that! I wasn't a prostitute! He simply responded by saying, "Where are you gonna go? Your family doesn't want you. You give it away for free anyway and look where it's gotten you, NOWHERE! And besides, what kind of mother would you be if you can't even pay for your daughters pampers?" That was all it took. Knowing nobody wanted me, nobody cared and I had to take care of my daughter. I felt I had no other choice.

It was not long after that I found out that the woman in Reggie's room was not his sister but his "bottom bitch". She was the one that he trusted. It was her job to keep all the other "hoes" in line.

She had his back no matter what. She was the one to teach me everything I needed to know about "the game". She told me whom I could and could not "date". Black men were a definite no! She let me know that if I ever see another pimp never ever look them in the eye. I learned quickly to walk across the street and not get in his path or he could "charge" me and take the money I had and the consequences would be a major beating. She taught me how to put a condom on so the trick wouldn't know I had used one on him. She also taught me that condoms are a must. If the trick didn't want to use a condom....no deal, no matter how much money he offered. This might be the only rule that my pimp had that I am thankful for. For the trick this was about sex, but for my pimp and therefore for me it was all about money. And the money went to my pimp. The bottom bitch also was my business coach; teaching me the basics like charging more for those who wanted more and most importantly to always get my money first.

I can still remember that first night so clearly. I remember the first "date" I had. He wanted oral sex, I didn't get to pick or say no. For $20 I climbed into his car, Ebony was right there with me. I was so disgusted as I was performing oral sex on him. He was so gross, he smelled so foul that I nearly gagged. I wanted to be anywhere but in that car doing what I was. I had to do this for my daughter; there was no one to help us. I got through it by thinking about taking care of my baby girl while struggling to comprehend how my life had sunken so low. When he finished I had to hold back the urge to throw up. I kept thinking I would have the money to care for my daughter. Caring for her was my priority no matter the cost. The first night was so surreal. As soon as the trick was finished Ebony had us out quickly and we were on the hunt for my next "date". Ebony was with me on every single date that night. At the end of the night I was devastated when I had to give everything I made to Romero. I didn't know that was a part of this. I did all the work; why did he get all the money? Ebony explained that all the money goes to Romero and he keeps a roof over our head, clothes on our backs and food in our stomachs.

We stayed in Miami only a few nights. We went into clubs, fancy hotels, as well as the streets. Wherever Ebony went, I had to go with her while my daughter stayed with Romero. We worked all night and would go back to our hotel before sun rise.

After a few days Romero decided it was getting too hot in Miami with the police so it was time for us to move on. He packed us up and headed to D.C. Romero had family in DC so once we got there he took my daughter to his family; to ensure that I wouldn't run. I can't even tell you how long my daughter was kept away from me. I felt trapped, helpless and hopeless; I didn't even know where she was. It felt like I would never be able to escape. It was not long before the guilt and shame felt consuming, what kind of life could I ever have now?

Life had become worse than imprisonment. The walls didn't have bars and locks, but walls and locks are not need to control a person when your child is held and your humanity is reduced to life controlled by a pimp. Night after night I had to go out and sell my body and hand over every penny made to my pimp. Ebony was with me almost every step, almost overshadowing me to ensure I wouldn't leave. She was his bottom, the one he "liked" and trusted the most. She was the one that he shared a room with.

Remember this was my dream guy. I literally and overnight went from giddy girl to his whore. I never felt more worthless than I did in this season. The realization that Mr. amazing never saw or heard anything more than a desperate, lonely and scared girl who was an easy target for him was as demoralizing as it was devastating. The truth was he saw nothing more than an easy opportunity and unless it was to collect "his" money he never gave me the time of day!!!

I was in a town where I knew no one, no family and no friends. I was allowed no outside contact unless I was out on the track. Since I didn't always meet my quota I didn't get days off. According to Ebony and Romero I didn't deserve days off.

I worked, in the cold, in the rain and at times in the snow. I remember one particular night, (but generally speaking days and nights lost significance when hope died.) It was a rainy Monday night; with very little traffic one of the few that Ebony was not with me. I guess she stayed back because it was such a miserable night. I had been out for a while and not made any money when a car finally pulled up. I got in after we agreed on price and we headed to the hotel. When the car stopped at a stop sign, a guy opened the door and jumped in next to me and as soon as he was in, the driver sped off!!! Fear was my first and immediate reaction!!! They took me out of the city into a rural area. Before we got to our destination both of the men had raped me. It's still somehow different in my mind, this night was clearly rape but while I now recognize that every instance on the street was rape there was still a difference. This difference, in my heart, is something I will be working to understand and step out of as I continue to heal. I remember one of them asking his friend, "Hey do you have any condoms? I want to make sure I don't catch anything from her." Now if that wasn't degrading, I don't know what is! This night I was grateful that they at least used condoms. I didn't want to catch anything from them or get pregnant.

They took me to a house where their friends were having a party and I was set up to be the party favor. I couldn't believe they actually took me back from where they picked me up. I was unbelievably grateful because they had taken me about 45 minutes away. Grateful faded quickly after making the phone call to let Romero know what had happened to me. His response...." you better stay out there until you have my money!" I expected he would take care of me, or be upset for me, but obviously there was no sympathy going on here! When I did get back to the hotel I found him pissed off at me, instead of the jerks that gang raped me. My punishment for being so stupid, as Romero put it, was a beating. I had to endure his violent beat down and insults, after being gang raped and then spending more time in the rain and cold to make my quota so that I had the right to go back in for the night. With each punch he would call me something different and degrading; a stupid whore, dumb bitch, a nothing piece of trash... I had to take the beating without shedding a tear or making any noise because tears and noise meant the beating got worse. I lay on the floor being stomped and punched like I was an animal.

Another reason that pimps liked going to DC was that the police didn't give the girls a whole lot of problems. One night while I was "working", I was approached by an undercover police officer.

Typically, if we saw a police car as long as we started walking they didn't really bother us; so when this undercover continued to approach me I was scared of jail and scared of the beating for getting arrested. This is another night that stands out, but for very different reasons. This undercover cop wanted to "save" me, not because he wanted anything in exchange, but only because he genuinely cared. He told me that he could tell I wasn't like the other girls and in his opinion I didn't belong out there. This cop gave me hope back, but I really wish people would understand that no one belongs on the streets or living as someone else's property.

The first time he approached me I was too scared to talk to him so he handed me his card and told me that if I needed help or anything to please call and he would help me. Of course as soon as I walked away I threw his card away because if Romero had ever found it I would be in huge trouble. The cop was persistent and continued trying until one day I finally talked to him. I told him how I ended up there and he said he could help me. He asked did I remember where my daughter had been taken and I told him I did so he pretended to arrest me and away I went. It wasn't too difficult to get my daughter back because who was really going to argue with a cop!!!!

My daughter and I stayed at his house for about a month before I decided to go back home to Miami. I have to say that not once did he ever attempt to disrespect me in any way. He just wanted to help us and make sure we were safe. I will forever be grateful to this man for stepping up and doing his part to help me get off the streets.

Love is found, Or Is It?

People tend to think that life is wonderful for survivors the moment we are "rescued". In the real world however that never happens. That moment of "rescue" is so misleading, it is, in truth the beginning of a new kind of fear with some big obstacles to navigate. Those obstacles begin the instant we leave, or escape the situation we were held captive in. While rape, torture and trauma bonds are, in actuality, more devastating than you can fathom this personal hell becomes the only reference for normal and stable many survivors have. The instant we leave we lose everything we knew as stable. To be free and safe we often must leave the relationships that while unhealthy and potentially deadly where also our protection and our family. The phenomenon of trauma bonding is more complex than most who have not experienced or lovingly supported someone through understand. Those who think they are coming to rescue us often come with their own pretty messed up superhero complex and typically fail to understand the complexity of the trauma survivors have endured. While "rescue" or leaving the extremely complex and violent trauma that survivors call everyday life is an essential first step, it is important to recognize that leaving is one of the bravest and boldest things we have done. It is nonetheless the first baby step towards restoration.

Yes, I was out and I had my little girl, but I had nowhere to go. I had no supportive community to fall into while I healed. I had no plan. And even worse than that, after all I had already been through, because I never felt safe enough, I had not experienced any healing or restoration. I had no reference to hold onto that said healing was a possibility for me and I had no idea what healing was even supposed to look like. So yes, I was away from my pimp, but I had nowhere to go, no one to help me while I put the pieces of my life back together and no one to show me the possibilities life offers, outside of trauma. It wasn't like I could move back in my dad's house especially after the trauma I was just rescued from. At that time I believed that I had managed to prove my dad right....I was nothing, garbage, lower than dirt.

So here I was, back home with no money, no job, no transportation and no place to live. I did stay with a friend until I was able to move into a women and children's shelter. My now rescued life was not feeling or looking like rescue; I was emotionally tormented, consumed by my pain and anger. I lacked self-esteem, and exchanged confidence for self-loathing. Rescued left me alone, broke and unable to support my child.

I believed that if I could find a man to take care of my daughter and I, we would be OK. Looking back, I couldn't have been more wrong.

The shelter required that residents be actively looking for

work. I mean really how realistic is that? My life had been hijacked, as a little girl and from then on the trauma just kept piling up and getting bigger. I couldn't function, I did not know what rational, non trauma thought patterns or beliefs sounded like, but okay I will look for a job, because apparently my worth as a human is directly connected to what I produce, or at least that was the way I internalized their rules. One afternoon while I was waiting on a bus for an interview, an extremely good-looking man approached me. He definitely had a large personality and was extremely funny. Just in that short initial meeting he made me laugh a lot and kept telling me how beautiful I was. His pick-up lines were really corny but they worked for me!! I was already awe-struck that such a good looking; funny man would be interested in me.

Over the next couple of weeks, we spent quite a bit of time together. I was already falling very hard for him and he said he felt the same way. I was able to really be myself around him. I felt so comfortable with him and felt that I could tell him anything. I told him all about my childhood, all my hurts, my dreams and aspirations. In feeling so comfortable I decided to tell him about my time in Washington D.C. and that I had been with a pimp. For a minute I thought that he would turn me away and never want to see me again but that was not his reaction at all!! He was elated and then dropped the bomb on me....he told me he was a pimp. My heart sank. I really didn't want it to be true but it was. In my mind I didn't want to be in that lifestyle again but another part of me didn't want to be without this man. At first he didn't push but he told me all of the reasons why I should be with him. He told me that he loved me and he wanted me to be with him. He talked about all of the money that we could make together. He made it sound so glamorous.

Over the next few days he really wanted me to make a decision. I didn't want to do it but I melted every time I was with him. Grudgingly, I finally told him that I wanted to be with him and would do anything he wanted me to do. I went back to the shelter, packed up my daughter's belongings and mine and moved into the hotel with him. I was right back where I started from but I was convinced that I was with the man I loved and that he loved me too. I was too hooked to leave, so I stayed and I stayed for about three years. Although I knew deep down in my heart this wasn't the lifestyle we needed to be in I took on the mentality that women give it away for free so hey...at least I get paid for it. I had to justify living that way and that was how I could justify it and live with myself. It's not as if I could've gone back to my dad's house. I was determined to never go back, no matter what! Besides, I had sunk as low as I could go and now the only person that wanted me was Smokey.

One of the things that Smokey attempted to teach me was how to steal and I am here to tell ya...there are two things I am horrible at, stealing and lying. He said that if I could steal it would be more money for us! It just wasn't going to happen...I always got caught!

I pretty much worked 7 days a week, 365 days a year. There were no holidays, benefits or paid vacations. I went to jail more times than I can count and my life was in danger every day. Being with the men that purchased me was degrading. Instead of living with the man I loved I lived life from rape to rape over and over again day after day after day. Every rape was a deadly risk, each trick I turned started with the terror and dread of wondering will he kill me, rob me, or beat me.

One particular incident still leaves me with chills. I got into a "tricks" car and gave him instructions to the hotel we worked out of. When I noticed he wasn't going where I told him to I commented that, "This isn't the way that I told you to go!" He smacked my face so hard that one of my contact lenses came out. I was in a panic! I wasn't sure what to do, I attempted to grab the gearshift and throw it in park but he hit me again even harder. He then pulled out a knife and told me "I better do as he says or I would die right then". My mind was racing as he drove. "Is this it?" I thought. Is this how I'm gonna die? He drove to a remote wooded area and made me take off all of my clothes. He violently raped me in ways that I had never been abused before and then announced that he was going to take me home to his wife so I could be their sex slave! I went in survivor mode, putting on the act that it all felt good and I couldn't wait to go home with him and meet his wife. I didn't cry, I didn't scream out, I knew that if I was going to stay alive I had to play along with him. After what seemed like eternity he started letting his guard down. I watched as he placed the knife in between the seats and kept on playing the role, waiting for an opportunity, and when it came I was able to grab the knife. I had a split second to react or die. I made my choice trembling with fear as I snatched the knife and stabbed him in the chest. I dove out of the car and ran as fast as I could. In that moment I was a terrified little girl fighting to live. I just ran, not knowing where I was or where I should go, scared that he would catch me and my life would be gone. I didn't know or care if I killed him. I knew I had to live! I had no clue where I was but I knew I had to find the highway.

I was naked, scared and lost running through the woods and my heart was pounding so hard I thought it might burst out of my chest, waiting for him to catch me and kill me. I ran for what felt like days, I didn't think I would ever find the main road. And then finally, I found it, one of the main roads!! I kept running naked on this busy road. Surely someone would stop and help me but nobody did! Didn't anyone find it strange that a woman was running down the road naked? Finally, there was an auto shop down the road and I saw some men running towards me with a blanket. As soon as they reached me they threw the blanket around me and I just fell to the ground. I cried and was shaking so hard as I told them what happened. They offered to take me to my hotel but I was terrified this was just another setup. I finally agreed and got into one of their cars and all the others followed to make sure I got there safe.

As I settled into the seat and began to let myself consider that maybe I was safe my thoughts turned to Smokey. The last time I let something like this happen my pimp beat so badly I was left in a heap on the floor. Now I feared that Smokey would beat me up for not bringing any money home? Was he going to make me go right back out and work? There are no words I can give you to convey the level of unbridled terror and confusion I experienced throughout this ordeal. I knew I had just escaped a deeper place in hell, I didn't know if this stranger was going to take me home or hurt me and I couldn't anticipate how Smokey would react. I was an emotional wreck. I was relieved when I actually made it to the hotel. Smokey and some of the other pimps were outside as we pulled up and the men that brought me there explained what happened. Smokey thanked them for bringing me back safely and he proceeded to come get me out of the car. I really hadn't expected what happened next. He was actually concerned and worried about me. He took me to our room, held me for a while and told me to get cleaned up while he got me some food and let me know I could stay home for the night.

I was so relieved! And yes, I fell deeper in love with him, because he took care of me that night. No one had ever been there to take care of me after I got hurt, let alone brutally raped. I felt like he cared about me and that he loved me. How could I leave this man? He didn't treat me the way Romero did. I was so completely played and manipulated that that there was nothing I wouldn't do for this man.

During my time with Smokey I took my share of beat downs mostly because I had such a smart mouth and didn't always know when to be quiet but the worst one was when he thought I was trying to leave him. I had made the suggestion of working for an escort service instead of the streets because I was tired of going to jail and the crazy nuts that I was encountering. He took that as a sign that I was leaving him. He asked me to meet him at his other house and when I got there the fight broke out. He smacked my face so hard that I fell to the floor and didn't move. There was a very thick crystal vase that he grabbed and started beating me with it. The first few blows were to my back. He just kept hitting me over and over and I sat there on the floor with my knees bent, arms around them and kept my head down so he couldn't hit me in the face anymore. My daughter sat on the couch watching all of this, crying and screaming for him to stop hurting her mommy. It broke my heart! I don't know what hurt worse, the blows I was taking or hearing my little girl scream and cry the way she was. I just knew I was going to die as my daughter watched. I also took several blows to the head and legs. I was so bloody and all I could hope for was for him to stop. Relief finally came when the police came banging on the door. The neighbors had called the police because they heard him yelling and my daughter screaming. The police asked if I wanted to press charges and I told them no, I just wanted out of there.

They offered to have an ambulance come and get me but all I wanted to do was find a place to clean up and go to sleep so they took my daughter and me to a shelter for battered women. I swore I would never be with him again. I was going to get a "normal" job and have a "normal" life.

The next day I was in so much pain I knew I needed help and medical treatment so I ended up in the ER after all. By the time they saw me I had waited too long and was told they couldn't stitch the wounds on my head or shin. I left the ER with crutches to support my leg from the severe bruising on my shinbone, my wounds cleaned and bandaged and my back so bruised that you could not tell what color my skin was!

I was absolutely never going to see him again!!

As the bruises healed and the lonely nights got worse, I called him. I missed him. I LOVED him. He said he was sorry! He said he needed me! He said it would never happen again! (And how many times had I heard that?) And yes, I went back to him again. But when I went back there was something different. I just could not go back into this life. I couldn't bear to live in this shame and degradation anymore. I think he knew it too and suggested for me to go to Memphis and see his mother and take a break and I did just that.

When I got to Memphis his mother's house was being renovated so I was unable to stay with her. I stayed at the Salvation Army and that's when I met Angela. She was my roommate and was running from her pimp. We talked and dreamed about her going home and me getting a" real job" and a new start. Why do so many survivors think in terms of real job verses turning tricks? Think about it turning tricks is hard, emotionally devastating and physically debilitating work. The fact that we don't get to keep the money or that it's not an acceptable job does not mean it was not real or hard, hard work! I held onto my dream and actually did get a job. My starting over seemed like a real possibility this time, my job was due to start in a week, but I never made it to that job.

Kidnapped

Angela and I went everywhere together. We even met a couple of guys and started hanging out with them. For a brief moment it felt like maybe hell had actually frozen over and we were going to get to live our dream. Little did we know that these *nice guys* were friends with Angela's pimp. One minute we were all laughing, having a great time, the next minute these guys come in and start dragging Angela out the door. I was petrified! Her pimp looked at me and said, "I know a hoe when I see one, I guess I'm getting two for one!!" His friend grabbed my daughter and as I ran out the door, there was a gun to my head and I had no choice but to get in the car with them. I was so scared!!! I didn't know anybody, was in a city I knew nothing about and now had no way of calling anybody that I did know! The fear was very overwhelming. I didn't think I was going to make it out of this alive!

The first night was spent in what almost seemed to be an abandoned apartment. It was filthy, disgusting and reeked of urine, stale cigarettes and weed smoke. We slept on mattresses on the floor with no covers. This had to be a dope house. Angela took quite a beating that night for running away and there was nothing I could do to help her. The next morning, we headed to California! The drive was long and horrible. All we heard Bones & Spike talk about was pimpin' and how good the "pimp god" was to give him back his hoe and another one! All I could think of was how I was going to get away and get back home! That first night in California was a nightmare. Since we were in the area where Angela was from she called her dad and he came and got her. On one hand I was happy for her to get away but I was the one that suffered the consequences and I found myself being angry because now I had to deal with this crazy man alone! I took a really hard beating because she left. Bones said it was my fault she left and I should have called him but I didn't know she was leaving; she just never came back. This man's beatings were like no other beatings I had ever endured. He was the type of abuser that would make me get in the shower and while I was still wet and naked he would beat me with belts and hangers. The pain of each hit with the belt was like fire, it stung on my wet skin and was so painful but I was not allowed to cry out or else he would do it more for acting like a baby. He said a real hoe doesn't cry, she takes the beatings like a true hoe is supposed to.

One of the hardest parts of this was that my daughter was in a separate hotel room. Bones felt that I wouldn't be able to leave if I didn't have access to her. He would allow me to see her if I met my quota but punished me by not allowing me to see her if I didn't meet quota. He was making escape extremely difficult. I was stuck; there was no way out, no hope! Was this how I was going to die? Or even worse, was this how I was going to live the rest of my life?

Crack had hit the streets and Bones did both heroin and crack. I however was not allowed to do any drugs because I needed to be able to support his habit. Now I couldn't even cope by numbing. When I didn't make quota he would accuse me of getting high and I would have to endure one of his beatings.

I remember one night I was out and it was a very slow night and I didn't make any money. He was furious! He told me that his pimp friends said their girls made plenty of money and I must have either been getting high or giving it away for free. He made me take off my clothes and get in the shower and then while I was still wet from the shower he took a clothes hanger and started beating me with it! The pain was horrific! The clothes hanger was even worse than the belt. I could feel not only the firing sting but the blood as it dripped down my back and legs. When he was hurting himself with the hanger he decided to stop and just kept punching me like I was a useless piece of meat! The blows were too much for me to endure. He punched me everywhere he could get to, my face, my stomach, my arms and he kept screaming at me for being a useless whore. He accused me of stealing from him and raged about killing me because I wasn't even "worth being a hoe". As if my self-esteem wasn't low enough now I had this psycho telling me I wasn't even good enough to be a hoe. I was not a pretty sight after this beating. My saving grace was his friend Spike that had been with us telling him to stop and that I wouldn't do him any good all bruised and hurt.

One night while I was out it was extremely slow and I knew the one definite rule was to never date a black man but I was desperate. The reason for this was because most pimps felt a black man were not as "quick" as other races therefore it was totally forbidden. But I knew the consequences of not making quota and I didn't think I could endure another beating. This black man was offering $100 and I couldn't pass that up!! So we got a room but as soon as we got in the room I noticed he was putting on gloves and I was immediately in a panic. I ran to the door but he got to it first. He then grabbed me by my throat and started to choke me. He dragged me to the bed by my throat and I could feel my life slipping away. I fought so hard but he was so much stronger than I was. I even grabbed his testicles and squeezed as hard as I could and pulled on them as hard as I could but it didn't faze him. It really pissed him off that I was fighting back and not submitting but I wasn't going down without a fight. He flipped me over on the bed and brutally raped me. That pain was so unbearable but because of all the beatings I had already endured I had learned to keep my emotions under control and go to another place in my head. On this night my ability to dissociate was gone, I can look back and see how not dissociating allowed me to fight and kept me alive. The entire time he raged like a wounded lunatic about his sister who was killed by a trick. He promised to even the score by doing the same thing to me! All of a sudden he just stopped and ran out the door. I don't know why and really didn't care why, I was just grateful that he didn't take my money or my life.

I told Bones that a white man did this because I would have been severely punished if he knew it was a black man. He must have been in a good mood that night because he told me to just come in for the night even though I didn't make quota. I learned to play the game with Bones like I had learned to play by the rules and live with all the other captors and predators in my life.

My life was hell for the next few months. He was always moody because of his drug use. I took the brunt of his anger.

One night there was a knock at our hotel door. Since he wasn't there I looked out the window and saw it was one of his pimp friends so I let him know he wasn't in. When Bones got back to the room he found out that I had responded and was absolutely livid! (If you remember from earlier, we are not supposed to even look at another pimp let alone speak to them) He started acting like a crazy man! The beating I received that night was worse than any I had taken so far! When he started the assault we were in the room where my daughter was sleeping, so he dragged me by my hair down the hall to the other room we had and it got real ugly real fast!!! At first he started punching me it's hard to describe if you have never been beaten like this, but the punches were more vicious and damaging than normal. He was screaming about what a disrespectful hoe I was. Telling me how stupid

I was to respond and didn't I know that dude could have charged me for talking to him. He went into the bathroom and filled up the bathtub. Once full he dragged me into the bathroom and attempted to drown me. He kept forcing my head in the tub holding me just to the point that I thought I would pass out and die! He did that quite a few times and then he dragged me back into the room where he poured alcohol all over me so he could set me on fire!!! By this point in the assault I was so terrified that when he ordered me to look for the lighter I did. When he couldn't find the lighter he started to beat me again. The blows were devastating. I was in so much pain. The relentless assault went on for at least an hour. I suspected that I had some broken ribs and my face was an absolute mess. There was blood all over me from my nose and cuts from his punches to my face and arms. He was getting tired of punching me so he started beating me with a belt on my back and my legs. Finally, he said he was tired of me and was going to kill me and that's when he started choking me to the point where I blacked out! I woke up being surrounded by pimps that were telling him he had to stop because he was gonna end up going to prison. Not the fact that I could have died but only because he would get arrested!!! Once he finally got calmed down enough I couldn't believe he actually wanted to have sex with me after that! I reached my breaking point and had to find a way out!

The next morning, he kept saying he was sorry and that he wouldn't do that again, I was his moneymaker, blah, blah, blah!

I was in so much pain, every part of my body hurt. I could barely move but I was expected to go back out on the track that night and now looking back I was so glad that I did! I looked a hot mess. I was unrecognizable. My face was bruised, cut and swollen to the point that I looked atrocious. Who was really going to want to have a date with me that night? I was disgusting looking. I was bruised all over my body! But I went out and was immediately stopped by the police. They questioned me about who did this to me and I eagerly told them the entire story. I explained that I was kidnapped from Memphis and brought to San Diego by a pimp and he was holding my daughter in a separate room. I told them where he was and where my daughter was and they immediately went and picked him up. I had to wait with another officer until they could bring my daughter and have me identify him. It seemed like an eternity but finally I had my daughter in my arms and he was on his was to jail. They took me down to the station to give my statement and then put me in protective custody for a month. They paid for my lodging, food and essentials we needed during that time.

Then the court date came. I went to court ready to testify against him but he took a plea bargain and that was that. Next thing I knew my daughter and I were on a bus back to Miami.

Back Home

I had already made arrangements to stay with a friend once I got back and the first person I couldn't wait to call was Smokey. Despite what I had already been through, I was still in love with him, so why wouldn't I call him? That's the bottom line. When I called him I told him what happened from the time I left Memphis. He told me he heard I was with this other pimp and he thought I chose up (Choosing up is a term used when a "hoe" leaves her pimp and chooses another one). He had no idea I had been kidnapped. We agreed to meet up. I was scared, because I didn't know if he was setting me up for another beat down, but I was in love so I went. Thankfully there was no set up and we really just talked. He told me that he had another girl and I was so angry. How could he get someone so easily? I thought he loved me! I fought hard to be the only one because I didn't want to share him. He told me that I would always be his special one and that he loved me but she was making good money for him and she would take care of me too. I told him I couldn't do the streets anymore so he suggested working in strip clubs.

I was able to get an apartment and I then started working in a strip club. Smokey and his girl lived in a hotel close by and it was killing me. I was so jealous because he spent most of his time with her. I hated her. One day in a rage of anger because he wouldn't return my calls I went to the hotel he was staying at. I banged on the door but he kept telling me to go home. I got so angry that I started beating on the window and busted it. Hands bloody, anger raging I ran as fast as I could before the police came so I wouldn't get arrested.

Later that night he came to my apartment and told me that he only loved me and I had to understand that he was a pimp and I was no longer in the game and he wasn't going to leave the life. He also told me that they were leaving and going to Atlantic City where the money was. I was devastated. My heart ached so badly. I couldn't lose this man again. I cried and begged him not to leave but it didn't work. We spent our last night together and he was gone the next day.

I had never felt heartache like I did when he left. But he was gone. I was going to have to move forward.

I tried working in "white" strip clubs but because of the way I was built I couldn't make a living. I decided to try working in a "black" strip club and made better money, but it wasn't easy for a "white" girl to be in a black club. The other dancers didn't appreciate most of the white girls coming in their territory but I was able to fit in.

I was able to stand up for myself and didn't allow any of the other girls intimidate me. I wasn't the typical "Barbie" white girl trying to fit in.

I was getting high daily, and although I was making good money, I spent most of it on drugs so we moved quite frequently because I couldn't afford to pay rent. Buying powder cocaine was getting more expensive and crack seemed to be the thing but I was hesitant. At the time I was working in a real dump, which is where I met a couple of dancers who smoked crack all the time. I started sprinkling my cigarette with coke and convinced myself that I wasn't as bad as my 2 other friends. One night when I couldn't afford what I needed they introduced me to crack and I was hooked after that first hit. My life really took a nosedive from there. I moved in with my two friends and this man they lived with. In every house around us there was a dope boy. My 2 friends would sleep with them or perform oral sex in order to get their drugs but I refused to do that and somehow I earned respect from the dope boys because I wouldn't do that.

Across from us lived an older dope man and his incredible wife. She would babysit my daughter every night that I worked at the club. All of the dope boys in the area loved Davianna and would by her clothes, shoes, a bike, toys, anything she wanted. They did their best to take care of her. I wish I could say that I did the same. I was a horrible mother. When I would get angry I would lash out at her. She was such a sweet little girl and I treated her so bad. But even when I treated her bad she would tell me how much she loved me and I would feel so guilty. It was such a vicious cycle. I loved my baby girl so much but when I was getting high I was a monster. I would promise that I wouldn't get high anymore and then would feel guilty when I would get high again. After about 7 months of living in this place the dope boys stopped selling to me. They told me I didn't belong there. They said I was different than my 2 friends. They would tell me how much my daughter needed me to get right and I would just cry. I was so broken and that was the only way to mask the pain. After about a month I moved from that area and never smoked crack again but I still got high on cocaine.

In between all the different moves Smokey somehow always found me and kept in touch with me. He ended up going to prison for murder. He got into a fight with another pimp trying to defend himself. He was unable to enter a plea of self-defense and he was given a long sentence.

His girl was still working for him and sending him money so he was taken care of and wanted to make sure I was ok. He told me his mom had passed and I was very sad to hear about that because she was an amazing Christian woman and incredible example at a time when I didn't know God.

A Crazy Marriage

While working in the last strip club I worked at (and I worked at many) I met my first husband. He would come in every night and supply me with all the cocaine I wanted. I had started drinking because alcohol balanced out the high so I wasn't so jittery and I could actually function. It wasn't long before I moved in with him but there was always drama with his daughter's mother. He had custody of their daughter and I was convinced that he was going to save me. He actually had a legit job and was making good money and just sold dope on the side. Compared to the men I had known so far, he was a dream, or so I thought. What I didn't know is that he had a sex addiction. He wanted to be able to have a woman that was ok with him sleeping with other women, not away from home but together. I was so broken and craved loved so much I agreed to it and he married me. One of the girls at the club was my best friend and she was the one he picked. He made sure to keep me high and drunk so that I would do whatever he wanted. It wasn't long before she moved in with us. Her boyfriend was killed leaving her an emotional wreck, which caused her to lose her apartment.

She had a newborn at the time so I couldn't see her out on the streets and my then husband was more than happy to have her move in. That's when things got really crazy. I stopped working at the club because I wanted to get my life together. So during the day while I was at work he was sleeping with her and at night while she was working at the club I was sleeping with him. I needed him to make a choice between her or me. I was his wife and I wasn't having it. She started calling and threatening me while she was at work telling me I better not be "sleeping with her man"! Her man? Really? He was MY husband! This was getting way out of control. During Hurricane Andrew it was insanity at our household. While the hurricane was going on I was in the living room with the kids while they were in the bedroom. She threatened that if I even thought about coming in there she was going to whip my ass. How had things gotten this far? After the hurricane was over I had walked to the store to get some beer since I couldn't get anything stronger. When I got back I saw the baby in the living room and heard them in the bedroom. That's it, I had enough! When they came out of the bedroom I went crazy! I was like a lunatic. I started beating on him and he pulled me outside for to talk. I called my sister and told her I was going to jail because I had enough and I was gonna kill him. I had him pinned up against the fence wailing on him. All the frustration I had with him over the past year I took out on him that day! While I was whoopin him his girlfriend called the police. Unfortunately, my sister and the police pulled up at the same time and she couldn't save me from going to jail. He said that he didn't want to press charges but in a domestic violence situation the State takes over the charges. So off to jail I went. He did come bail me out but everything had changed from that point. I was sick and tired of being sick and tired.

I was sick of the drugs, I was sick of the drinking and I was sick of being with crazy men so while he was at work, I packed up mine and my daughter's things and left. I had a friend that was in recovery that said I could stay with them until I got on my feet.

Recovery

September 21, 1992. I will never forget that day. That was my very first day clean in 6 years! I went to my first Narcotics Anonymous meeting that day and went to meetings every day for 6 years. I stayed extremely involved and watched my life change without drugs, I got my GED and my driver's license not long after getting clean but there was still so much drama in my life, **because I hadn't changed**. My father got sick just before my first year clean. He had been sick for a while with emphysema and had gone blind as well. I went to see him two weeks before he passed and for the first time he told me he loved me and that he was proud of me. I was sitting in an NA meeting when I got the call that he had passed. I felt so many emotions. I was sad because he was my father and I loved him, I felt anger because I didn't think he suffered enough after all he put me through and I was even madder because he took all those secrets to the grave. Then I felt guilty because I was angry. It was such an emotional roller coaster.

I married a second time but that marriage didn't last long because he cheated on me with someone that had the aids virus. The fact that I was never infected is yet another way God protected me during these years.

As I was working the 12 steps, I came to the one where I had to make amends to those that I had hurt. That was a pretty long list. Smokey was one of those that was on the list. I found out he had been released from prison and was back in Memphis. I called directory assistance to see if he was listed and sure enough he was. He found God in prison but I had seen lots of people go to prison and find God only to walk away once they are released. I really didn't know what to expect when I called. He was stunned when he heard my voice. I told him why I was calling and he said, "Are you crazy"? "I'm the one that needs to make amends to you for all that I did!" He went on to explain that he no longer goes by the name Smokey because that was the old him and to please call him Theodore. He genuinely loves Jesus and had turned his life around. He had a real job which he had held for some time, his own place and he did street ministry every Saturday. I was astonished! We talked for hours and then again frequently, but I wasn't sure about this "God" stuff.

Meanwhile my life was still in turmoil. I was in relationship after relationship and wasn't happy. I was still picking men who were toxic and abusive and getting hurt emotionally and physically in each relationship. While I was working at a nail salon in Ft. Lauderdale I met this client who came in every two weeks and would talk about God. She invited me to her church several times and while she felt different than I had experienced Christians to be, in my head I believed that the church would blow up with all that I had done and seen. I was too evil for church. I had done too many bad things. I could still hear my grandmother's voice telling me that I had sinned and I was going to hell and there was nothing I could do about it. That same woman came in every two weeks for a year and just showed me love until I finally I gave in and visited her church.

I was amazed when I walked in. It was held in an elementary school cafeteria and everyone was dressed in jeans and very casual. I felt the spirit of God that day and continued to go every Sunday. I loved it so much and even more I loved how I felt that I made the decision to get baptized, soon after. I had never experienced feeling good about me, let alone the hope and Joy I was feeling. I was so excited that I had my neighbor and best friend Sharon and her kids coming with us as well.

Theodore

I was still talking to Theodore every day and it seemed as if God was connecting us together somehow. He wanted me to come visit him in Memphis and I put it off for quite a while because I didn't know if it was a trick. I loved him but I was done being used and hurt. I was done long before the hurt and abuse stopped because, I, like so many had no idea how to take back the rights to my body and life, let alone what a healthy relationship looked like. Deep down inside because of our history I was very much still afraid and waiting for the next beat down. It took a long time and so many long phone conversations but I finally agreed and he sent me a plane ticket to come see him.

When I arrived I was so nervous. It had been years since I had seen him. I was pleasantly surprised how the trip went. He was such a gentleman and he really was a changed man. We prayed together, talked a lot about God and he shared all he had been doing. We were in the process of getting ready for church when we realized we both had the same exact color on. We kept seeing these different signs that we, in our immaturity and the twisted confusion of our history took as signs that God was somehow orchestrating things, we just weren't sure how.

We went to his church and he did something that just

blew me away. He stood up in front of the entire congregation and shared his testimony and proceeded to apologize for all he had done to hurt me in the past. I was instantly in love with him again. And to this day that is my standard for what change looks like. If your man tells you he is sorry for beating and using and then goes back and does it again he is not sorry or changed, but if he stands up in front of an entire congregation and repents and tells you he is sorry the change may be in the process but it's likely real. That took a kind of courage and manhood I had never witnessed before, it doesn't, on the other hand, take any courage or manhood to lash out emotionally or physically. I don't think the love ever went away, but it did change into something authentic and real. As I was leaving we said we would pray about what the future holds and allow God to move instead of our emotions.

When I got back home I was making some real decisions. I didn't want to stay in Florida anymore because it just reminded me of all the turmoil, drama and trauma I had endured. I didn't know where I wanted to go but my emotions kept saying Memphis. I called around looking for an apartment, in Memphis, and was approved before I got here. I of course took that as a sign and assumed another indication that God was bring Theodore and I together. I do believe I was supposed to come, but not to be united with Theodore.

My visit to Theodore was in November of 1998. He came to Ft. Lauderdale and spent Christmas with me and on

December 27th, 1998 he helped me drive with all my stuff to Memphis. God was really with us on that drive because we drove on a donut the whole time. I stayed with Theodore for a couple of weeks until I could get a job and in to my own place. As I said earlier he was a complete gentleman. From the first time I met him after prison we both agreed that sex was off limits. Once Jesus found me and I began living by his standards for how a woman deserves to be treated it became even more important that we live godly lives with no sex before marriage. Staying with him allowed me to see that as hard as he was in the street was how hard he was about God. I was a new Christian with so much to learn about Jesus, truth and myself. He expected me to change overnight which wasn't real or possible and we didn't make it together too long. Change and healing are a lifelong process and never happen based on demand, no matter who demands, or how much we want change. Both require time and work. I needed to find a church to help me settle in, I started searching but Theodore was set on me attending this one particular church. It was so big and I wanted a small church like the one back home. I learned quickly that smaller churches, in the south, weren't fond of me having a mixed child and therefore weren't very welcoming. I finally gave in and went to the church that Theodore told me about. The first Sunday I was too late for service but I took a bulletin and saw two things that attracted me. The first was that they offered an anger management class and the second was a dinner on Wednesday nights with your first week free. Those two things were the deciding factor for me.

A New Man

I was in my apartment, had a decent job, and was now involved in church but I was still miserable and empty inside. The folks at the church were nice but I didn't feel like I fit in, those old beliefs about being too bad held tightly to my heart keeping me on high alert waiting to be tossed out. One of the pastors introduced me to a lady that had a black husband and felt like we would hit it off because that's what we had in common and we did. As time went on I was getting behind on my bills and ended up taking on a second job at a nightclub as a waitress. Now everybody knows that when you are in recovery a bar is NOT the place to be because eventually you will take a drink and that's exactly what happened. It was not long before I left the church and found myself in yet another bad relationship with a married man, convinced that this one was different and the one that would save me. Once again I found myself on a downward spiral that could end only in me self-destructing and crashing. Life was crazy and revolved around being in a relationship with a married man, drinking continuously and creating a horrible relationship with my teenage daughter. I had put her through hell multiple times and just as she felt like maybe we were getting some stability I was taking us back into crazy and taking my anger out on her. My drinking made it even worse. At my lowest point I was drinking a pint of Hennessey every night. While I worked at the club I would stop by the liquor store and get a double shot of liquor so I could drink at work. I kept this up for about a year and thats when I met Keefe (my now husband) I was out with my neighbor at her uncle's birthday party and there he was. I knew he was watching me because I was watching him on the sly. We started talking that night and I gave him my number. His cousin told me about what a good man he was and a hard worker and he would be good for me. So I ran with that.

Our very first date was epic! He wanted to make sure I was dressed for the occasion so we went to a boutique and he bought me this amazing gown with all the accessories and shoes to match. We went to see Morris Day and the Time at one of the casinos and had a ball!! It was amazing. I never had a man treat me the way he did. I honestly didn't know how to take it. It wasn't long before we moved in together. But boy did I take him through some changes. I had been through many stages of getting out and getting sober, including becoming deeply aware of the devastation known as my temper, but none of that was actual healing. I had a lot of baggage that I brought into this relationship. I did however bring one good thing into the relationship. I knew I needed to get back to church and most importantly back to Jesus with who I first experienced hope and joy, for the first time. When I asked him how he felt about going to church and said he grew up in church and so off we went to find a church. There was a new pastor taking over the church I had attended previously and I really wanted to see if he was a good teacher. So we went and I loved the pastor. He taught in such a way that I could understand. Keefe got involved with sound and I got involved with the choir. I just knew that this time I was going to change.

I don't know whether I was afraid of how the relationship was going or if I was really feeling condemned that we were living together and that was a sin in Gods sight but I told him that he had to leave and we could date but no sex. I was sabotaging the best relationship I ever had. He was not a happy camper. So he packed up his stuff and he left. He didn't want to talk to me and I dont blame him. I made him leave his apartment to move in with me and now I was putting him out. He thought I was psycho and looking back, I really was. He had no idea how deep the trauma scars went into and around my heart; I had not let him into that place. He also didn't know about a lot of my past and therefore couldn't possibly understand that I was trying to live a normal life without any understanding of what normal or healthy looked like. I love and adore him and even still it is hard for me to find the words to help him understand why something's are so big for me or why I sometimes react so differently. Now however it is not because I am needing to keep secrets to hide my shame it is my heart's desire for him to understand and know my heart fully I just still don't feel like I know enough about normal to put something's into words that make sense, to the man that loves and adores me.

Despite what to him must have seemed irrational at best we got back together and June 6, 2002 we got married. I still had little healing or working on understanding me, my past or the beliefs about myself and relationships left behind by a life time of trauma. I of course, believed that everything would be perfect, now that we were married. That belief was based in fantasy land, and inside I remained miserable and alone. Looking back, I am able to recognize that I was the problem, but at the time I blamed everyone else. I had serious anger and control issues. I was not an easy woman to have a relationship with. I would argue with him and he would get up and say, "You can argue by yourself." He would literally walk away from my arguing and leave me alone to fight with myself which infuriated me. I would get up and follow him to keep the argument going. When that didn't work or I didn't get my way I hollered louder and threw things. He had what he called the "Kelley kit" which consisted of plaster and paint to fix all the holes I put in the walls.

Over the next 4 years' things got progressively worse. I placed all blame on him. I felt like he thought he was better than me because he was mister goodie 2 shoes. I felt like the folks at church thought they were better than me. I saw me as a bad person who had so many issues and dark baggage. My self-perception and insecurities helped push me away from church. The church I picked ended up being unhealthy and I was hurt and spiritually abused by the staff. I finally realized that life had molded me into a different person. While I was becoming more self-aware I didn't need people treating me different. It took some time for me to realize that the way I was being treated was not okay. When you grow up with abuse and neglect as your norm it often takes a while to realize that the situation is wrong verses the belief that I am bad. As a result, it frequently takes longer to leave bad situations. Such was the case with the new church, but I did leave.

I felt like nobody saw my side or understood why I was upset with Keefe and in their eyes he could do no wrong. We tried counseling a couple of times but it felt like I was the person who always needs to change or who was wrong. I didn't stay with counseling very long as a result.

My husband is very laid back and he doesn't let things bother him. He is very mild mannered and is always calm. I took his easy going nature as a weakness. I was so used to thugs in my life that I did not know how to handle or communicate with him. He loved me but I couldn't see it because I didn't love myself. So one day, when he took his son to college, I packed up and left and moved in with my daughter. He called me later that evening and asked me if this was what I truly wanted and with an attitude I said yes and that was that.

Another Downfall

It did not take long for the drinking to start. Drinking, misery and loneliness all automatically went together back then. And, needless to say, I ended up in a very toxic relationship. This time I recognized the signs but figured if I loved him enough he would change. That never happened. For 2 years it was like being a prisoner. I wasn't allowed to drive my own car, I paid for everything, I was constantly being accused of cheating which seemed ludicrous considering I couldn't go anywhere alone. The relationship started with the rosy honeymoon stage but turned ugly fast. He had a phenomenal sense of humor leaving people laughing all the time but it just helped him hide his out of the world temper and violent jealousy. I remember one-night I disagreed with him, over something simple. He went ballistic and started accusing me of not having his back, which progressed to the you don't really love me game, ending with a reminder about going against what he said, all that after I expressed a different opinion.

During the same time, I started school to get my Tennessee license to do nails. One night when he picked me up he said he saw a guy getting out of a car while he was waiting for me and accused me of cheating. Of course I wasn't but he didn't believe me. A couple of months later he claimed he saw that same car at the salon I was working at and he said he knew I was cheating on him. I tried to explain that it belonged to an older lady that worked there but he didn't believe me. He slapped me so hard that I ran out of the apartment to try to get away from him but he caught up to me and slammed my head into the brick wall. I thought I was going to pass out right there. I am still amazed I didn't get a concussion. He dragged me back into the apartment and beat me for running. No one in the house tried to stop him, not his sister, brother, nobody! They would just look at me pitifully like they couldn't do anything. The next morning when I woke up he must have busted a blood vessel because from the back of my ear down my neck, all around the side of my neck to the front was nothing but a big bruise. It was so embarrassing going to work looking like this. That's when everybody knew he was abusing me. I started showing up with bags under my eyes and my giggly personality was gone. I was so stressed. I was constantly walking on eggshells not knowing when he was gonna flip out.

A little over a year after I left my husband he showed up at my job with divorce papers. I was stunned to see him and especially with divorce papers. I signed them and as he walked out the door took one more jab at his heart, "Easy come, easy go!" I was so coldhearted. I know that response was really in reaction to the abuse and hell I was living through again, but it still hurts when I think about how I treated him, back then. I never meant to hurt Keefe the way I did.

The last straw came when I found myself 40 years old, on the floor being kicked like a piece of garbage by this man crying out in pain with him standing over me with a machete. I could do nothing but lay on the floor and beg God, to show me what was so wrong inside that I left a good man to get beat up again.

Not long after that we got our own apartment. I was not allowed to go anywhere accept to work and church. And I swear he had the house bugged. I was doing nail clients on the side and had a conversation with one of my clients and later on he asked me about the conversation. He was into having tiny cameras and gadgets around.

Christmas of 2007 was a disaster. I made sure I got him so many gifts that I knew he would love! I cooked a big Christmas dinner, invited my daughter and grandkids over and was so excited for him to open his gifts. So I had everyone sit around the living room and I passed out the gifts. As I was giving Damien his gifts he proceeded to go off on me. He started screaming at me asking me did I think he was a child? I told him "No, why would you ask that?" We were having such a good time and I couldn't understand. He said, "You don't give adults their gifts at the same time you give children their gifts. Its disrespectful and you are trying to insinuate that I am a child." My daughter tried to reason with him but that seemed to infuriate him even more. He left out of the house without even opening his gifts. It ruined the whole day and I was so scared that entire day because I didn't know what he was going to do to me.

When he finally came home later that night I drove Davianna and the kids home and she said to me that if I needed her just call and we would use a code word and she would come right over. When I got home he played an audio of exactly what we talked about. I was petrified. I made sure all the knives were out of site and prayed for God to keep me safe.

He was pretty upset to know that I would call the police, considering had a record. He called me all kinds of B's and H's, told me "it's no wonder your dad wanted nothing to do with you". His barrage of verbal insults ended with his telling me I was "not much of a Christian" and stating it's no wonder" my husband didn't want me because I wasn't marriage material".

I knew I had to leave. I had to start planning on how I was going to escape. I came to the realization that I had a good man and didn't even see it but he had moved on and was dating someone else. I asked God to please help me to get out before the New Year because I didn't want to bring the new year in with Damien. God answered my prayer, a few days after New Year's Day. On January 5th 2008 I was getting ready for church. Normally I left the house first, on this day for some reason he left first. I took the opportunity.

I packed what I could and left. I made sure I changed my phone number so he couldn't get in touch with me. I prayed and asked God, "Where do you want me to go?" his reply, "Time to go back to your home church."

PART 2

A NEW

BEGINNING

Free at Last

Freedom, for the first time in my life I felt free. The first thing I did when I left was change my cell phone number. I knew that I needed a clean break. I didn't want any contact from Damien. I still had so much fear of him that I didn't want to risk my safety. He still knew where I worked but I knew I would be safe there.

I had everything I owned in my car, no place to go as of yet and I just drove towards the area where my church was, but I had to make a stop first. I hadn't had a hair cut in months because Damien wouldn't allow me to go anywhere by myself. So, I went to Supercuts and while I was there my daughter called to check on me. "Mom, where are you?" So I told her, "I'm at Supercuts getting my hair cut." I hear her laugh and she said, "Let me get this straight, you have all your stuff in the car and no place to live and you're getting a haircut?" "Well, yeah, I gotta look good!" We both laughed hysterically. She told me, "Only you mom."

After texting my friends and letting them know I had a new number and that I finally left Damien. My dear friend Delana asked if I had a place to stay and I told her I didn't so she said I could come stay with her and her husband until I could get on my feet and get my own place. I am forever grateful to them. They were the perfect refuge and welcomed me in their home as if I was family. I thanked her profusely and told her I would be there after church.

As I pulled into the parking lot of my church that I had abandoned 2 ½ years earlier my heart raced. So many questions were going around in my head. "What if I'm rejected?' "What will Keefe think when he sees me?" "How will I be treated?" But as I got out of my car and headed into the church I felt like I finally made it home. I felt safe. I felt Gods presence all around me, reassuring me that no matter what, He was with me and I was going to be OK.

It was still early when I got there and I immediately looked up and saw Keefe in the sound booth. I walked up the stairs and as I approached him I saw this stunned look on his face. I walked right up to him and as if nothing ever happened I said, "Hey, how are you?" Still with the stunned look on his face he responded, "I'm good, how are you?" I shared with him that I was doing pretty good and made small talk with him and then out of the clear blue I said, "Well, can I get a hug?" Oh my God, what was I thinking? I had walked out on this man, hadn't spoken to him in over 2 years and I ask for a hug? Was I crazy? But, being the gentleman that he is, he gave me a hug.

It was getting time for service and since it was a Sunday night service I knew it wouldn't be too packed so I sat on the front row. I was going to get the word with no distractions. I was determined to give my all to Jesus. But I have to tell ya, I got more than one stunned look when everyone saw me. Some were happy to see me, others not so much. But I didn't care; I was home, right where God wanted me to be.

The next 3 weeks were spent making amends to the pastor and his wife, friends that I had abandoned when I left, working and really doing all I could to stay safe. At work it was difficult because Damien would call me constantly and his calls would leave me in so much fear. I was always looking over my shoulder. One call he would tell me how much he loved me and the next phone call he would call me everything but a child of God. Then the unthinkable happened. He showed up at my job. When I walked out to the service drive my heart dropped to my feet. My whole body was shaking. My stomach was turning and my mind was racing. Surely he wouldn't hurt me at my job would he? No, I don't think he was that crazy. There were way too many men around and the mechanics would have beat him down in a heartbeat, but still, there was that fear. As I stood there trembling trying to keep my composure Damien was sure to be on his best behavior, laughing and joking with a couple of the guys but all the while staring at me in a way that made the fear even worse. He finally said, "Hi honey, I have missed you so much." He sounded so sincere to others but I knew what he was really thinking was, "You better be glad all these people are here or else I would beat the hell outta you." He tried to find out where I was living and I just simply told him at a friend's house. He wanted to talk privately but I stood my ground even though I was shaking like a leaf and said, "We really have nothing to talk about, I'm done." I told him I had to get back to work and thankfully he left. Shaken and petrified I walked into my office and broke down in tears, not because I missed him but because the fear was so overwhelming. Surprisingly, I didn't get any more phone calls for the next few days.

Towards the end of January, I was ready to move into my apartment. I had no furniture except for my nail table but I didn't care, I was in my own place. Gratefully I did get some furniture from my friend Delana. She had some items in the garage that she didn't need or use so I was grateful for whatever I could get. I knew God was providing.

It seemed as though my life was coming into some kind of order but I constantly had this fear that Damien would find me. Although when we were together he always said that he wouldn't ever come into the area I was currently living in because it was too "white" for him but I feared that his rage would take over if he was drinking and getting high and he would take the risk and come find me. I did all I could to keep myself busy in order to escape the fear I was feeling. But for me at times that meant drinking to escape the feelings. Yes, even though I had rededicated my heart to Christ I was drinking to numb the pain.

I would feel so guilty going out to the Mexican restaurant with my friends Saturday nights and then going to church on Sundays but I wasn't going to miss whatever message God had for me to hear.

I finally got the courage to ask if I could rejoin the choir at my church and of course I was told they had to make sure it was OK with Keefe first since we would have to deal with each other because he was running the sound. I was grateful that he wasn't trying to keep me from what I enjoyed and that was being able to praise and worship. So now I had to see him every Thursday night at sound check and Sundays for church. I couldn't help but see him because from the stage I would be looking up at him as he was doing sound.

I was determined to change. I couldn't continue my life as I always had because my way clearly never worked and for the first time in my life I didn't need a man to validate me. I was OK being single. Just God, and me I was cool with that. I knew that I had sabotaged the only real relationship I ever had and he had moved on and was dating someone else. And to be honest, I didn't go back to the church for Keefe, I went for God.

It wasn't long before Damien started calling again and it was really making my work environment very difficult.

I was getting stressed all over again. The last phone call we had he told me "Bitch you better watch your back because when you least expect it I will find you and kill you. I now understand why that dude chopped up his girlfriend and stuffed her in garbage bags. You are nothing but a lying, cheating whore and I will kill you." And with that he hung up. I was frantic! I was back to shaking so hard that I couldn't even get my work done. I was crying and just a wreck. I didn't know what to do or where to turn. I couldn't even pray. This darkness came over me and I truly believed he was going to come through with his threat. Everywhere I went I watched my back. As I drove I would watch the rear view mirror to be sure I wasn't being followed. Instead of trusting God to take care of me I was imprisoned with fear. I allowed it to take over my life. I was in my own prison and it didn't feel good. With the phone calls continuing it really affected my job. I was arguing with this nut when I really should have just hung up on him but it had been 3 months already and I was getting tired of it and my anger was at an all-time high! While I was dealing with all of this commotion I had a coworker that really wanted my job and did all she could to get me fired and it finally happened.

My initial reaction was anger but the more I thought about it I realized it was a blessing in disguise. I no longer had the stress of the job or Damien calling. Although it was a good paying job, it was stressful. I had constant headaches and was always on edge. I have to tell you that when I woke up the next morning, it was as if a weight had been lifted. True I was now unemployed but I knew God would make a way and he did!

One of my passions since I was a little girl was the beauty industry. I love all aspects of it especially nails and makeup. I have had my manicurist license since 1993 and I decided that I was going to pursue it full time. I already had clients that I was doing on the side so why not do what I love. I felt that God was telling me to talk to Keefe's barber that managed a barber/beauty salon and that's what I did. I think he was a little apprehensive at first because he didn't want it to be an issue with Keefe but he finally agreed. I was so happy doing what I loved. It was hard work building up my clientele but I didn't quit or give up. I knew God had a plan and I trusted Him to take care of me.

I continued being at church every time the doors opened. I wanted more and more of God and I wanted to continue to grow and change.

There were many times I didn't feel like I fit in with these "church" folks but I refused to give up. It wasn't about them; it was about my relationship with Christ. I no longer cared who judged me, I was going to be faithful in my walk and if this was where God wanted me then that's where I was going to stay. I was desperate for more of HIM and less of me.

Now I have to be honest when I say I was by no means perfect. Although I wanted more of God there were some real struggles. I didn't really want a man in my life but I did feel that loneliness of companionship. I wanted that closeness and love but I wasn't ready. I would drink on the weekends to numb the lonely feelings and I had started back smoking cigarettes again. I am so grateful to my friend Amanda. She loved me where I was at and helped me get through those difficult times. She was one of those friends that I had abandoned but we got through that and she stuck by my side when nobody else did. She understood the pain I was going through and the struggles I was dealing with. She never judged me but always loved me. I know God placed her in my life at just the right time and for so many reasons. Truth be told, if it weren't for her Keefe and I wouldn't be back together now.

My Boaz

As I expressed earlier, I didn't go back to my church for Keefe. I went back because that's where GOD wanted me. But little did I know HE had a plan. I knew before I came back to the church that Keefe was dating someone. I didn't know how serious it was but I did see her attending the church. It didn't bother me at first but then it happened. It was about a month after I came back on a Sunday morning. We were both exiting the church at the same time and as he held the door open for me he said, "Well hello Mrs. Alsobrook." My reply, "Uh, hello." We really hadn't spoken at all during that first month because I wasn't around him much. But something happened when he spoke to me and I looked in his eyes. That feeling in the pit of my stomach, my heart started racing and then panic set in. "OH no, this isn't possible", I thought to myself. "NO, NO, NO" my brain screamed. All of this was happening in my brain as I walked to my car. "There is absolutely NO way this can be happening! This has got to be a trick of the enemy to get me off the path God has for me." I sat in my car, gripped the steering wheel with all my might and balled my eyes out. I cried out," GOD HELP ME! Surely, this isn't love that I am feeling!

Help me to be strong and fight this. The enemy knows my weakness is to have a man in my life but that's not what I came here for! God, I need your strength!" And then I heard it plain as day, "But he is you're covering just as Boaz was Ruth's covering." I sat there stunned and then said "No God, I'm serious, I didn't come here for that! I came back to this church for YOU!" And again I heard, "But he is you're covering, just as Boaz was Ruth's covering."

I cried all the way back to my apartment and the first thing I did was call Amanda. Amanda was not only my dear friend but stayed Keefe's friend as well while I was gone. She was there for him through his pain when I left. She knew how he felt and what his life was like after I left and how he felt about his relationship. The best part about our friendship is she understands me so well, in my good times as well as ugly times. She was the person I talked to about everything I was feeling even before I left Keefe so she knew the two of us very well. I called her up and said, "Amanda, you are not going to believe this." So I went on to explain what happened in the parking lot at church and what God had told me. She was stunned. I asked her if she thought I was just imagining things or could this really be happening.

Could it be possible that I would get a second chance with Keefe? She said, "Kelley, if God said it then its gonna happen." "But what about this relationship he is in?" She simply said, "It's not as serious as you think, but I do believe before you can start a new chapter with him you will have to get closure from when you left. You can't move forward until

91

you close the past." I knew she was right but how in the world was I gonna do that when he barely spoke to me.

A couple weeks later that opportunity came. It was after sound check on a Thursday night and as we were leaving I asked Keefe if I could talk to him. I expressed that I really wanted to get some closure from when I left. He was very reluctant but finally agreed so we sat in my car in the church parking lot and I poured my heart out to him. I apologized to him for how I treated him while we were married and the way I left. I explained what I had been through after I left him and all of these emotions came pouring out. I cried as I spoke to him but he wouldn't even look at me. He looked straight forward and didn't move a muscle the entire time I spoke. I told him that I wasn't trying to mess up his relationship with Ophelia. I paused to see if he would say anything, but nothing, complete silence. My last words to him were, "I feel like God is going to bring us back together."

As soon as I said that he spun his head around so fast to look at me and simply said, "I've gotta go," and he opened the car door and left. I sat there in tears. What had I just done? Now he really thinks I'm nuts. I just sat there, stunned and in tears. I whispered, "God if your plan is to have Keefe and I back together, you better tell him that because it's not looking so good from what I'm seeing."

I was on a mission. It didn't take long for everyone in the church to know that I wanted my husband back, including

Ophelia. It seemed every time I turned around there she was. She had even switched Sunday school classes to be in the one that I was in. She was really getting on my last nerve. But I held myself together and continued building my relationship with God. I was very involved in the choir and I was not going to keep my focus on Keefe because I wanted to be a better me.

Keefe and I really didn't speak much after our talk in the car. We were cordial and said hello to each other but not really too much beyond that. I continued to work at the salon, go to church and home. I was feeling so lonely and was being patient in what God promised.

One Thursday night after sound check Keefe asked if I wanted to go get something to eat with him and of course I said yes! I was so nervous, I had butterflies in my stomach. I wasn't sure why he would all of a sudden want to take me out to eat. Could it be that God was letting him know that we were supposed to get back together? I had so many thoughts running through my head. When we first got to the restaurant I was so uncomfortable because I really didn't know what to expect. We were both quiet at first and then started making small talk but as dinner progressed we started to open up more. Keefe told me how much I hurt him when I left. How broken he felt but at the same time he learned one very important thing. He explained to me that he had put me before God and that was a huge lesson for him. He knew that nothing was supposed to come before God. That night a lot of things were released and a heaviness and uncomfortability were lifted between us. That night brought a new beginning. We were able to get out a lot that needed to be said. I left that night with new hope. I knew God was working on Keefe's heart.

Of course when I got home I called Amanda and told her about dinner and she was elated!

She told me to stay patient and trust God. We talked about him still dating Ophelia and she said "Kelley, it's not what you think. He is not happy. He doesn't want this to be serious but she is wanting more from him that he is not willing to give." That gave me even more hope!

The night before my birthday I went to the Mexican restaurant to get something to eat and ran into my ex sister in law, and guess who was with her. Yep, Ophelia! Now when I was married to Keefe his brother's wife and I had some tension but that night she hurt me more than she could ever imagine. She hugged me and said it was good to see me and then she said, "Kelley have you met Ophelia? You were my sister in law but she is my for real sister in law." I was devastated! I felt like I was punched in the gut. I was angry and hurt but I kept it together and simply said, "yes we have met." I was crying as I went into the restaurant and sat there by myself and cried and drank. I got so drunk that night. I didn't know how else to ease the pain. I felt like a knife pierced my heart. The staff at the restaurant knew me and tried to console me but I was heartbroken.

My initial thought was that Keefe must have decided to go deeper into the relationship with Ophelia and maybe even asked her to marry him. My brain was in a whirlwind of thoughts. Of course I can make things much bigger in my mind than they really are. I assumed the worst. I knew I couldn't call Amanda that night because I was so drunk and didn't want her to be disappointed in me. So I just went home and cried myself to sleep.

Here it was, my birthday and time to go to church. I didn't want to face Keefe that day or see Ophelia. I wanted my day to be a good day not one of sorrow. God was going to get me through this ache that was in my heart. As I was driving to church I noticed a truck that was selling puppies. I immediately pulled over and fell in love with the cutest pit bull. He was the runt of the litter but I had to have him. I told them it was my birthday and I wanted to purchase him as my gift to myself. We were making arrangements to meet later because I certainly couldn't bring my new puppy to church with me when this car pulled up. When I saw who it was I thought, "Are you kidding me? What is SHE doing here?" It was Ophelia.

She called me over and said, "Kelley I am so sorry about what happened last night, I didn't think she would say that to you." I told her it was OK and it wasn't her fault. She asked me, "are you buying a puppy?" I responded, "Yes, he is my birthday present to myself." Apparently she wasn't a big fan of dogs, especially pit bulls because she just turned her nose up, said happy birthday and drove off.

Church was amazing and I had my best friend Amanda there to support and love on me. I told her what happened the night before and she couldn't believe it. She kept telling me, "Kelley it really isn't what you think it is. It is not a serious relationship and Keefe has been trying to get out of it." She continued to encourage me and just love me where I was at.

After church things got real interesting. I was on my way home and I saw Keefe was at KC getting something to eat, I pulled in to the parking lot and we talked for a few minutes. He explained he was sorry for how my ex sister in law acted the night before but her and Ophelia had gotten close. He told me Happy Birthday but that because of his integrity, he didn't want people to get the wrong idea if we were seen together.

He has always been a one-woman man since I met him and for people to make assumptions about us it really bothered him. Well, wouldn't you know it, our pastor pulled into the drive thru as we were talking. Keefe was not happy about that because he felt it made him look bad. Everyone knew he was dating Ophelia and here he is talking to his ex-wife who has clearly made her intentions known. I was on a mission to get my husband back. He said he had to go and I said that I needed to go get some items before I picked up my new puppy anyway.

I left feeling broken hearted once again and cried out to God, "God I thought you said he was my Boaz? Did I misunderstand you? Nothing is showing me any hope!" Do you think God answered me? No, dead silence. I was so confused at this point and was ready to give up all hope of Keefe and I getting back together. Ok, I was gonna shake it off and just move forward. It was clear that it was going to be just me, God and my new puppy, Chocolate.

Just when I was resigning myself to the fact that I must have heard the wrong thing from God, Keefe pulls up next to me as Im walking to my car one Sunday morning and hands me a book and says, "Read this." And pulls off.

No, "Hello, how ya doin?" Nothin! The name of the book was "Love and Respect: The Love She Most Desires; The Respect He Desperately Needs" by Dr. Emerson Eggerichs. As I was reading what the book was about I was dumbfounded. In a nutshell, this book reveals why spouses react negatively to each other and how they can deal with conflict quickly, easily and biblically. So now I was REALLY confused. Why would he give me this book and tell me to read it? Of course as soon as I got home, I called Amanda! That poor girl, she had to endure all of my craziness but I am so grateful to her. I explained about this book and she was as puzzled as I was but again she told me, "Kelley this relationship between Keefe and Ophelia is not what you think. He is not happy." Here I was, once again full of hope. I did read that book and I learned so much from it. I was so convicted as I read it because I knew I had mistreated Keefe when we were married. I did all of the wrong things this book talked about. I belittled him, made him feel unappreciated, talked crazy to him, and outright disrespected him. I gained a new understanding through this book about how men and women have totally different needs and as these needs are met, the marriage will become a healthier, happier marriage.

Things started to become very chaotic at church with friends that weren't just friends with me but also with Ophelia. I had some people tell me I was overstepping my bounds and that I needed to leave Keefe be. They told me I already had my opportunity and I blew it so just let it go. I was being made to look like the bad guy and I had to defend myself. I wasn't the only one who played a part in this. I was told that I had my chance and that I needed to leave him alone, but what they didn't realize was I wasn't "Chasing" him. I didn't call him, I didn't even have his number, I didn't chase him down at church to talk to me but if he approached me in any kind of way I wasn't going to let it go. But I knew what GOD told me and that was who I was going to believe in. People could be mad all they wanted. At that point I didn't really care what people thought. It got so bad that Keefe called me and said "Kelley, you know I'm dating Ophelia and I'm not the type of man that cheats." I started balling my eyes out. This was it. My hopes were shattered. He then said something that puzzled me. He said, "Kelley I need you to be patient and I need you to be strong. Read between the lines of this conversation." OK, now I was really confused. What in the world was he talking about? Was there still hope? After our conversation I raised my hands and said, "God you take this, I can't do this anymore. You told me that Keefe was my covering just as Boaz was Ruth's covering and I believe you but I can't take this roller coaster ride anymore." And then I proceeded to call Amanda who was as confused as I was.

May 14, 2008, the day before my best friend Amanda's birthday. We had sound check that night and before we got started, I went upstairs to the sound booth and with an attitude I told Keefe, "Don't forget about Amanda's birthday tomorrow." And was getting ready to walk away when he asked me, "Where is your phone?" A little shocked by this question I asked, "Downstairs. Why?" He said, "I want to give you my phone number." And with quite the attitude I said, "What about Ophelia?" He said, "We broke up." OMG! At that moment I could have jumped up, screamed "Hallelujah, Thank YA Jesus!" and did the "Holy Ghost" dance. But I didn't, I really refrained myself. Very calmly I said, "Well, I will get it from you after rehearsal." In which he replied, "Well, I may be leaving early." I didn't want to seem too eager so I simply said, "Well, I guess I will have to get it from you another time." And I walked back downstairs.

Low and behold, Keefe stayed through the entire rehearsal and asked if I was hungry and for us to get something to eat. We dropped his truck off at his house and we rode in my car to the Mexican restaurant. We had great conversation and then it was time for me to drop him off. When we were married we had a black cocker spaniel named Ivory. So I asked him did he still have Ivory and he told me yes. I said, "Well, can I see her?" He said, "Yes, she's in the back yard." So I called her name and she was so excited to see me. Even after 2 ½ years she remembered me. So I then asked him, "Aren't you going to invite me in?" He said, "C'mon Kelley. But you know I have to be up early for work." My intentions were not to leave and I didn't!

About 2 weeks later I was able to get out of my lease and moved in with Keefe, dog and all. We did have some drama with Ophelia for a little while. She would show up at the house while Keefe was at work, show up at my job, leave stuff on my car while I was at church. It was crazy! I had really kept my temper in check and allowed Keefe to handle this because I knew my way would land me in jail. But she was really pushing my buttons and I allowed her to get to me.

Finally, one Saturday morning she came to my job and said, "I hope you and Keefe will be happy. I have decided to move back home. I met someone and I know we are going to be happy." I was so grateful she was moving out of state and out of our lives for good.

Now I'm not gonna sit here and tell you that Keefe and I getting back together was easy. For the first few months he would make snide remarks and remind me of what I missed out on by leaving him and it was very hurtful. At first I would let the remarks slide but then it got to be too overwhelming for me. I finally sat him down and said, "Honey, if we are going to make this work, you are going to have to stop throwing up my past mistakes in my face. It isn't fair and its very hurtful. I can't go back and change the past and I've apologized over and over again. I don't know what more I can do." He agreed and apologized and said he really didn't realize he was doing that and from then on he stopped making the snide remarks and we began to move forward. I still had a lot of insecurities to work through because in my heart I was scared that he would just put me out as a way of getting back at me for hurting him so badly. This was something that took me quite a while to work on and it took him having some real patience with me.

After a few months we decided that we were going to get married again. We went back to the jeweler that made our original rings to pick out an engagement ring. I told him I wanted something unique. The jeweler said, "Well, I may have the perfect ring. I made it a year ago and haven't shown it to anybody and I'm not sure why, but I will show it to you and see if you like it." When I saw it I fell in love with it!! It has a blue sapphire in the middle with diamond baguettes on each side. I later realized that Keefe's birthstone is Blue sapphire and mine is diamond. That ring was especially made for me and the jeweler didn't even know it! Another sign.

We decided that we didn't want a big wedding, just something small and intimate with a couple friends so on Monday, March 23, 2009 we got married for the 2nd time in a small chapel with Delana and her husband and a couple others as witnesses. But we did have a beautiful reception a couple weeks later.

There are so many things I love about my husband but one of the biggest things is that he doesn't try to change me. He allows me to be who I am and grow in my own time. He doesn't nit-pick at every little thing that I do and he encourages me in everything I do unless he feels that it will harm me.

He knows when I need my space and he gives it to me. He knows when I just need him to hold me and let me know things are going to be ok. We have been through many trials together but we have gone through them together. He has truly been my rock and knows how to very calmly reel me back in when I get crazy. He doesn't have to yell or call me out of my name or put his hands on me to calm me down. When I am in one of my moods or am getting a little crazy he simply looks at me and says, "Really Kelley?" in a calm voice and that usually brings me back down where I need to be. He has been there for me when my nail salon folded, through deaths of loved ones, through my hurts and pains as I have been healing, my physical limitations, PTSD and so much more. When I feel like I am being a burden he tells me, "Honey, we will get through this together and I've got your back. If I didn't love you, I wouldn't have married you twice."

It's funny because we are total opposites. We are like night and day (literally) but we complement each other so much. Where he is weak I am strong and vice-versa. He is laid back and calm, nothing ever bothers him and I'm the high strung one. He is the behind the scenes type of person, while I'm in the spotlight and the social butterfly.

We don't even agree on sports teams and football season is particularly funny in our household. But what we do agree on is that we love God first and we love each other. I could never imagine my life without him. As I am writing this, tears are welling up in my eyes because of how grateful I am that God handpicked Keefe just for me. God knew exactly the man that I needed in my life to help me heal and know what true love really is. He truly is my Boaz.

Changes in the Church

I remember this Sunday morning like it was yesterday. The entire congregation came in as we always did expecting the great sermon and teaching that was to come but we were in for a huge shock. Our pastor had announced that he was offered a position at another church out of state and he was leaving in 2 weeks. It felt like I had just been punched in the gut. There was no replacement for him and he was just going to up and leave in 2 weeks' time. The emotions that took place in me were crazy. I was angry, disappointed and devastated. Our pastor was a great teacher and I learned a lot from his teachings. We weren't really close but I need that teaching. How could he leave us like this? He was just going to abandon us like that for a mega church? Did we mean nothing to him? His wife was our choir director and she was absolutely amazing! She didn't just sing, she truly worshipped from her heart and now he was just going to take that away from us?

The next six months were so chaotic. We had no lead pastor and way too much drama going on. I told my husband it was time for us to look for another church and he said, "No honey, this is where we belong. God has a plan, just be patient."

I didn't want to hear that, but I knew deep down in my heart he was right. It seemed as though the drama would never end. Every time we turned around something else would happen that was devastating to the church. My faith in the church and "church" people had really left a sour taste in my mouth. Every Sunday and Wednesday I would just go through the motions and I felt like my walk was getting a little stagnant. What I forgot was that God had a plan. And oh what a plan HE had!

June of 2009 there was announcement one Sunday morning that we were interviewing a potential pastor. His family was coming to Memphis for a meet and greet as well as we would be able to hear his vision for the church and ask him questions and then we as a church body would vote whether we wanted him as our lead pastor. At first I had no intention of going because at this point I felt so betrayed by pastors that I looked at them as I do politicians, all talk and no action. But at the last minute I decided I was going to go, just to see what lie he was going to tell us. His name actually peaked my curiosity, Matt Anzivino. Me being Italian, my initial thought was, "Hmmm, he's clearly Italian so how bad could he be?" I know, ridiculous right?

I attended the meet and greet and saw the family, of course Pastor Matt has this amazingly beautiful family. Gorgeous wife, 2 beautiful daughters and even his son was good-looking. I immediately judged them by their looks. I thought to myself, "great, we have the perfect little family here. I bet they have the white picket fence, dog in the yard and perfect life." Yes, I know what you're thinking. I was being extremely judgmental and you would be right. I was so hurt by the church already that I was very leery of what this new pastor was going to bring to the table. Would he make broken promises? Would he and his family be cliquish? Would he be understanding of my hurts and pains and the healing that not only I but our community needed?

Now picture this. Here I was, a couple of gold teeth in my mouth, braids with beads halfway down my back and still on the "hood" side and up walks this potential pastor, this short, Italian dude, clean cut, nicely dressed but not too dressy. He made a beeline straight towards me, reached out his hand, looked me straight in the yes and said, "Hello sis, I'm Pastor Matt. What's your name?" I shook his hand and very shyly said, "Kelley." We made small talk for a few minutes and before he walked away he said, "It's so nice to meet you Kelley." I was stunned! My brain was screaming at me, "Kelley, what was that? Where was your attitude? What just happened? That was weak! You folded!" But there was something about his eyes and the genuiness in them. He wasn't intimidated by me like most people were. It was almost as if he understood me in those first few moments of meeting me. It was something very unfamiliar to me. Not too many people "Get me" but he did. I had to get it together. I wasn't going to let satan trick me into thinking this pastor actually cared about my pain and my hurts.

It was time for us to gather in the main sanctuary to hear what Pastor Matt and his wife Shannon had to share with us. I was ready. I was going to pick out every flaw and give those negative check marks on why he didn't belong there. But God had a different plan. I listened intently as he spoke. He talked about where he came from and about the church he planted in North Carolina and that he felt called to come here and bring change to our city. Not just our church but the city. He shared his heart about the lost and was so genuine. Shannon shared how she was not a singer or the typical pastor's wife. She wasn't there to "Take over" ministries but she would work alongside us. She works a full time job as a nurse and she supports her husband in what he does with the church. Now that was different. Most of the pastor's wives I knew were always trying to make themselves known in the church but not Shannon. She was more of the background type of person. She didn't want to be in the spotlight. The one quality I saw in both of them was how humble they were. You can't fake humble. All of a sudden as I listened to them I started balling my eyes out. God was whispering to me, "They are real and I sent them here and they are the perfect ones for this church. Stop fighting." I couldn't stop crying. I knew that this man of God was really about "the least of these" and his heart was for the hurting. It was time for the church to vote and of course Pastor Matt was voted in as our new lead pastor. I felt a renewed hope for our church and its growth. I don't mean growth as people coming (which yes I wanted that too) but I mean our hearts and our love walk to grow and become unified in the mission of the church.

We had the honor of hearing him preach the next day and I have to tell you he has an amazing way of bringing Gods word into everyday situations. He shares in such a practical way that it's not hard to understand. He shares about his own flaws and also brings humor into his sermons and he's not afraid to step on some toes.

He cares about souls and wants to see everyone come to Christ. He lets us know that we aren't a cruise ship, we are a battleship. As believers we aren't supposed to just sit comfortably in the pews and just be glad about our own salvation but we need to have a heart for those that are hurting and need Christ. Pastor Matt is about bringing unity in a city that is so separated by race. Ours is a very unique church. We have every race and culture you can think of and while we have lost many of our "old" members we have gained so many new members that really have a heart for Christ and want to see change in our city.

One of the things I love most about Pastor Matt is that he is really a people person. He wants to know everyone that comes to our church. He's not one of those pastors that gets whisked away after a sermon. He is out in the lobby talking to the people in the church and most of the time his wife, Shannon has to pull him away and say, "Babe, it's time to go."

Over these last few years I have grown to love Pastor Matt as a father figure that I never had. He has always been there to support what I want to do to help women that are hurting. I am so grateful to God for bringing him and his family into my life.

Pastor Matt will never realize the depth of the gratitude I feel. He has always done all he could to let me know how worthy, loved, and special I am. He never judged me from the very first meeting and for that I am ever so grateful.

I Was a Victim?

Around June of 2011 I owned my own nail salon in one of the local malls and was friends with our districts State Representatives who was also set up in the mall. We were having a meeting one day when this woman came in telling him that he really needed to do something about human trafficking and that he needed to read this report about a website called backpage.com. She was sharing so much information about it that I was getting a little overwhelmed. Whenever I heard of human trafficking my initial thought was that it was a 3rd world country issue not an issue here in the United States. And honestly that's what most people think. I listened to Brenda as she spoke about what an issue this was in the United States and right here in Memphis. I couldn't believe what I was hearing! What? This happens here? She talked about prostitution and I really wanted to know more since she was so knowledgeable.

As she was leaving the State Representatives office I caught up with her and said, "I haven't shared this with anyone but I was a prostitute." We went into my salon and she asked me a series of questions. "Was this something you wanted to do?"

I replied, "NO, I felt like I had no choice." She asked, "Did you have a pimp?" "Yes, I had 3 different pimps and I was kidnapped by one of them.", I replied. "Were you taken across state line?" she asked. "Yes." She then asked, "Share with me how you started in prostitution." And I gave her a brief rundown on how I got involved. And then in such a loving way she said, "Kelley, you were trafficked, this wasn't a choice you made. You were coerced by the first 2 pimps and then kidnapped by the third." I sat there shocked. And then came the tears. For over 20 years I held on to a secret because I thought I was dirt, scum of the earth, no good and truly undeserving of real love. My mind was reeling with so many questions and everything started to make sense. It was as if a huge weight was lifted off my shoulders that I had been carrying for so long.

I started working with Brenda and her organization to be able to help other survivors. We had meetings at a local Starbucks every Saturday morning for healing with other survivors, some were domestic violence survivors, some human trafficking. I had already been supporting domestic violence organizations but this was the first organization that I knew of that talked about human trafficking. I wanted to learn all I could and help as many as I could.

In October we went to Nashville to speak in front of the women's caucus, these were some of the most powerful women in Tennessee. We were sharing about the importance of aftercare and shelters for human trafficking victims. For the first time I shared my story and how my life would have been different if I would have had the healing I needed when I got out of the life. I held my composure as I spoke but when I sat down after speaking I broke down. It was as if I was being released of this heavy burden the more I cried. I was mourning for the years I had lost, the years that were stolen from me. The heartaches and abuse I had endured for so many years. This was truly the start of my healing process.

As I drove back home, I made a promise to God that I would never stop sharing my story. I had finally found my purpose. I knew God had a plan and a purpose for my life but I didn't realize it was the trauma that I had endured that would give me that purpose. I was truly on a mission. And I'm still on that mission. I will never stop sharing about how God has turned my mess into a message. There are way too many women suffering today because of the secrets they keep.

EmpowerU is Born

I learned a lot about human trafficking with my time serving under Brenda but our season together was over. It was time for me to move on and start my own organization. I wanted to help spread awareness and help victims become victorious. I really wanted to be in the trenches and help those that were hurting so badly and in silence. I was amazed how many trafficking survivors were around the country. I made so many new friends through social media that are strong leaders and had survived some horrific trauma. They are now my sisters and that is a bond that no one will ever understand.

Until December of 2015, my organization was called Ashes2Beauty and I had put a Board together and we were going to get our own 501(c)3 but it wasn't in Gods timing just yet. Instead we became a part of our churches nonprofit and I was able to hold classes at the church and have events to bring about awareness of human trafficking. I have been able to speak at churches, organizations and conferences about human trafficking.

In November of 2013 I felt God leading me to start an internet radio show just for human trafficking survivor/warriors to share their stories. It would be a platform for them to use to share their experience, their healing process and what they are doing now to help others. When God first called me to do this I said, "God, I've never hosted a radio show! I don't know the first thing about doing this. Are you sure you want ME to do this?" But I knew this was what He wanted. My first few shows were a hot mess but I have learned so much and really love and have such a passion about giving survivors this platform. I have met so many amazing survivor/warriors and I'm so grateful for that.

In December of 2015 after much prayer I made the decision to rebrand. I spoke to many women, Christian and non-Christian alike and asked what was their first though when they heard Ashes2Beauty and the responses I received amazed me. I was told they thought of death and being called dirt. It was certainly not the response I expected and that's not the perception I wanted to give women. I wanted them to feel empowered, strong, worthy, loved and special and that is how EmpowerU came to be.

I felt God leading me to get our own nonprofit status but continue to partner with our church. The House Memphis will always be our home church but we are working on bringing churches together to help in the fight against human trafficking. I really prayed about who would be on my Board and God was very strategic about my Board members and I have to say I couldn't have asked for a better choice of Board members. We have so much we want to accomplish. EmpowerU exists to positively impact the lives of human trafficking and abuse survivors, while partnering with communities to become trauma and abuse informed.

Part 3

MY ROAD TO

HEALING

When I had left the last bad relationship I was determined that I was going to grow in my relationship with Christ. He was my saving grace and HE was the only man I could depend on that wouldn't hurt me. This part of the book I will share my experience in my healing and growth process. It is so important that when we have experienced any kind of trauma that we heal from it so that we don't bring the baggage of hurt and brokenness into other areas of our lives.

I struggled with seeking help via therapy. I didn't want to be put on drugs that would make me become a zombie but I found just the right psychiatrist that informed me I had been misdiagnosed as bi-polar for years and what I was struggling with is PTSD and anxiety. It made sense because I had been through my own war and was struggling with triggers and didn't even realize it.

Another thing I did was started networking with other "healthy" survivors. I was amazed when I started finding so many survivors on social media. Now I knew I was no longer alone. There were women out there that understood my "odd" way of thinking and helped me realize that I wasn't crazy but needed a whole lot of healing.

I am so grateful to my survivor sisters for being such a strong support system. And there are so many that are doing great things in this war against human trafficking.

One survivor in particular and what she was doing really

helped me to be able to dream and showed me that I can do and be anything that I wanted. Her organization, Rebecca Bender Initiatives, are really doing great things to help survivors to heal and even start their own organizations, businesses or whatever it is that particular survivor wants to do. Her book *"Roadmap to Redemption"* allowed me to really think back and get to the core of my hurts. She continues to be an inspiration in my life and to the lives of many other survivors.

The next few chapters will not only tell you changes that I needed to make within myself but will also help you grow and heal. Each chapter will have some scripture references as well as a "Self-Check" for you to write your thoughts and be able to walk through your own healing. My prayer is that my experience will inspire, motivate and empower you to walk in your greatness and allow you to see the amazing person you truly are!

SECRETS

Secrets can be very painful. I learned this lesson the hard way, by keeping some of my deepest secrets closely to my heart where I thought no one would see them, for over twenty years. I didn't want anyone to know about the physical, mental, emotional and sexual abuse I had endured since childhood. I assumed that since my family didn't believe me nobody else would. My shame and life experience taught me that I was responsible for what happened to me. I had some dark skeletons in my secret closet, but the biggest one was that I had been a victim of human trafficking. I didn't want anyone to know I had been with 3 pimps, worked the streets and later became a stripper. During that time, I was raped, beaten, belittled, almost lost my life several times, tortured, dismissed as unwanted and unloved. I believed, because I was told that being a prostitute was a choice that I made. I never considered that choice would mean I could walk out the door or take a night off without the fear of being beaten to death. I felt so dirty, worthless and full of shame and guilt. I felt that I would be unlovable, that I was "damaged goods". I held lots of anger, resentment, guilt and shame as a result of believing those lies. The words and labels I believed about me kept me in unhealthy relationship after unhealthy relationship. I hated myself and felt unworthy of real love. Heck, I didn't even know what "real" love was until a few years ago. I was so accustomed to being treated like garbage that I didn't feel I deserved anything better.

Fear was also a big part of my life. Fear kept me in trapped and most of these relationships as well as in the secret. It was as if I was living in my own secret prison I was afraid of everything and everybody. The fear was so overwhelming that I didn't want to open up to anyone I didn't want to reveal the secrets in my life. I continuously looked over my shoulder waiting for someone to take my life, or at least beat me down. I have been threatened on numerous occasions by ex-relationships that when I least expected it they would find me and they would kill me.

The sole purpose of this book is for women to be able to let go of those secrets that are festering deep down inside keeping you in bondage. I want you to know that you can be healed and whole by releasing those deep, dark areas in your life, they don't have to haunt you anymore. Whether it was from your childhood or a traumatic experience as an adult know that you are not alone and don't have to suffer in silence any more.

How many times do we as women hold on to secrets because we don't want anybody to know about our past? We don't want anybody to know what we've been through. We don't want anybody to judge us on that secret. It may be something like being molested as a child. It could be that you have been abused. It could be that you have been raped. It could be that you were doing drugs. Maybe there was infidelity in your marriage, lost a child or even had an abortion. Many of these things are true for me. I hid all of my secrets for 20 years and it killed me. I don't mean in the physical sense but I mean on the inside. I was dying on the inside. My healing process didn't really start until I learned to trust God. I had to allow God all the way into my life; which meant into my heart and yes even into my secrets. I had allowed Him in my life into certain parts, of my life, because I kept hearing these sermons over and over again "if your earthly father is this good to you then imagine how your heavenly father would be."

Well, my earthly father was not that great so when I thought about God as a father it was hard to trust Him. I didn't have a reference for a dad that was safe, protective, involved, nurturing or loving. It took time and effort on my part, but as I started to trust HIM because HIS love is unconditional I started releasing my secrets to him because I knew in my heart of hearts that he would never leave me or betray me. God sent his ONLY son Jesus to die on the cross for ME, but not only for me, he did it for you as well. Now some of you reading this may not want to hear about God but that's where my healing process took me.

When we hold on to these secrets, anger and resentment, and bitterness move into our heart and head and with time get bigger and louder. I know for me; I was such an angry person. When I finally broke free from bad relationships and finally started gaining healthy relationships I didn't know how to handle being treated with respect and honour. I took all the anger I had deep inside of me out on the ones who were really trying to love me. I was mean and hurtful to them because I had so much hurt on the inside. I was finally in a safe place and all I could do was unleash all the pent up anger that I had inside me because I knew that there would be no consequences or so I thought. I knew that my husband wasn't going to put his hands on me or even respond to my verbal assaults, so I thought it was safe to finally explode. I didn't realize that what I was doing to him was abusing him the way others had abused me, not physically but verbally and mentally. I threw fits every time I didn't get my way. I would throw things; break things, punch walls and act just like a crazy person. I was still holding on to the secrets, my husband didn't even know what I had been through, he just knew that there was something that was hurting me on the inside and did what he could to love me through it.

Here are just a few things that happen as a result of holding onto secrets.

- We stay in the bad relationships.

- We bury our pain. (or at least try to)

- We may not see it but that stuffed pain drives our emotions.

- We develop destructive cope patterns; like men, drugs, alcohol, stealing or abusing others.

- Secrets hold us in bondage; which becomes more entrenched the longer we keep the secret.

- We become physically sick as the stress and fear of the secret being discovered causes a multitude of health problems.

- We lose opportunities to have the things we want and need, because our need to keep the secret safe, forces us to stay silent or hidden.

- The secret becomes our identity and defines our view of self and potential.

- Often we lose healthy relationships and foundations because we view them through our secret self-perspective.

I did all of the above. I stayed in abusive relationships because it was comfortable. The endless pain that consumed my heart and tormented my thoughts left me hurting so deep I did drugs and drank like a fish to bury the pain. I stepped from one bad and abusive relationship to the next as quickly as I could find someone, driven by the little girl desperation to finally be loved. I convinced myself that if I could find a man who loved me he would take away my pain and leave me feeling instantly whole and content. **NONE of that worked for me and it won't work for you either.**

Pride is a major hindrance. If you allow pride to keep you holding on to secrets than you can't heal and you will stay stuck in the rut you are in. Would you rather be released from the hurt, pain shame and guilt or do you just want to save face and continue dying inside? Realizing the need to let go of the secrets and work through the associated shame is the first step. Realizing a need however does not mean that we understand how to let go or even what we need to understand so that the shame no longer ensnares our hearts. SO what do you do now? You are thinking, "I've got this one little thing that I swore I was not going to tell anybody." You've got to let go. Release it by sharing with someone you can trust. Share it with God, He already knows your secrets anyway so why not trust him to heal you?

I have to say that I am still amazed by how much changed for me when I started releasing the secrets in my life. I noticed that I was able to love better, and my anger was less explosive. Physically I felt healthier as the shame fell off. Healing and freedom felt somehow more real and solid without the secrets hanging over my head. I'm not going to say that it is an easy process but it IS a process. One I started sharing with those closest to me what I had been through; it was like a weight being lifted off my shoulders. I chose people in my life that were trustworthy, honest and real to share my secrets with in the beginning. I allowed people in but I was careful of who I chose to share these deep dark secrets with. I still had the fear of being judged but I was not going to continue.

Freedom. That's what the key is. We want freedom right? Well, God wants freedom for us as well. 2Corinthians 3:17 says "Now the Lord is the Spirit, and where the Spirit of the Lord is, there is freedom." God wants us to be free. He does not want us held in bondage. He wants us to be free, Galatians 5:1 says "For freedom Christ has set us free; stand firm therefore, and do not submit again to a yoke of slavery." I was in bondage. I was enslaved. Romans 8:1-4 says "There is therefore now no condemnation for those who are in Christ Jesus. For the law of the Spirit of life has set you free in Christ Jesus from the law of sin and death. For God has done what the law, weakened by the flesh, could not do. By sending his own Son in the likeness of sinful flesh and for sin, he condemned sin in the flesh, in order that the righteous requirement of the law might be fulfilled in us, who walk not according to the flesh but according to the Spirit." John 10:10 says "The thief comes only to steal and kill and destroy. I came that they may have life and have it abundantly." That does not say in a little bit of bondage, a little bit of freedom, a little bit of good life. He said have it abundantly. Are we living abundant lives? Are we walking in freedom? Are we walking in our uniqueness? Are we walking the way God intended us to be? We need to take God out of the box because He is an out of the box God. Isaiah 40:31 says "but they who wait for the Lord shall renew their strength; they shall mount up with wings like eagles; they shall run and not be weary; they shall walk and not faint." Like eagles! We stand on these promises. These are promises for freedom. Luke 4:18-19 says "The Spirit of the Lord is upon me, because he has anointed me to proclaim good news to the poor. He has sent me to proclaim liberty to the captives and recovering of sight to the blind, to set at liberty those who are oppressed, to proclaim the year of the Lord's favour." We are free. Are you walking in your freedom?

FREEDOM and BONDAGE

You may be asking yourself "What is freedom and why is it so important for me?" Let me first get into the definition of freedom and then we will talk about why it's so important.

Webster's (Merriam-Webster Dictionary, n.d.) **dictionary defines freedom as:**
1. The state of being free or at liberty rather than in confinement or under physical restraint: He won his freedom after a retrial.

2. Exemption from external control, interference, regulation, etc.

3. The power to determine action without restraint.

4. Personal liberty, as opposed to bondage or slavery: a slave who bought his freedom.

When we hold on to our secrets we don't have the freedom in our lives to truly move forward, heal and grow. We think if we just ignore the secrets it will go away but it doesn't. The best example I can give is if you take a beach ball and push it under the water what happens? It pops right back up again. It's the same way with your secrets, the more you try to push it deep down it has its way of popping back up in a way that keeps you from being free. It will eventually pop up back in your life in the form of anger resentment bitterness. You will be acting out in ways that too you seem not normal for yourself but it's just that hidden rage at hidden anger that keeps us from being free. We need to release the secrets in our lives in order to experience true freedom.

Once I was able to share my secrets I began to feel freedom in my life. The burdens or bondages of those secrets were being released one chain at a time! I had so many chains weighing me down that I was literally in bondage to the secrets that I held. I didn't want that for my life any more. I wanted to live free, not as a slave. I had been a slave of so many things for so many years that I was done. I saw people living free and I wanted that and you should want that for yourself as well. You may be sitting there saying, "Kelley, you just don't understand, so much has happened in my life and I would rather just forget about it. Nobody has to know." You are so wrong precious one. You deserve happiness, joy, freedom and so much more. I understand more than you can ever know. It's time to gain freedom from the bondages that are keeping you from moving forward.

So what is bondage you ask?

Webster's (Merriam-Webster Dictionary, n.d.) **dictionary defines bondage as:**

1. Slavery or involuntary servitude.

2. The state of being bound by or subjected to some external power or control.

3. The state or practice of being physically restrained, as by being tied up, chained, or put in handcuffs, for sexual gratification.

Here are the ways bondage will affect you. You will stay stuck in unhealthy relationships. I can tell you that I grew up in abuse and I didn't go through a healing process so what did I do? I picked men that were just like my dad. I stayed stuck in unhealthy relationships. I didn't tell anybody that's what I was going through. I didn't care. I just wanted somebody to love me. I equated sex with love and I equated getting beat up with love because I didn't know any better. So I held on to it and I held on to it. I didn't release that secret so I stayed in really bad relationships. What bondages are you holding on to?

Then there is the victim mentality. You may be asking yourself, what is victim mentality?

Webster's (Merriam-Webster Dictionary, n.d.) **dictionary defines victim mentality as:** the belief that you are always a victim; the idea that bad things will always happen to you.

I have found in my own life that I was so busy walking

around blaming everyone else for all of my problems. Everything that went wrong was somebody else's fault. It was never my fault. I never took responsibility for my actions. I never took a look in the mirror and asked myself; "what is it that I'm doing? What part am I playing in what's happening in my life?" It wasn't until one day as I was laying on the floor being kicked and beaten by my abuser as he was holding a machete in his hand threatening to cut me up in little bitty pieces that I finally asked myself, "What is it that's still in me that I need to work on that allows me to keep allowing people to treat me like this?" It was on that very day that I decided no more victim mentality and it was time to heal.

How many women do you see walking around with that victim mentality? Woe is me. Poor Me. Why does this happen? Why does that happen? Why do I get in these relationships? Why do I attract these same men? Well, you attract what you are. If you're not healthy, you're certainly aren't going to get someone who is healthy. How I got my husband, I don't know. That was by the grace of God. And I was crazy enough to leave him because I didn't know how to receive love. I left him for 2 ½ years and got into an abusive relationship where this man almost killed me. It was only by the grace of God that he married me a second time.

There are 2 major areas that will keep you in bondage and they are shame and guilt. So many times we blame ourselves for things that happened to us as a child, teenager or even as an adult. I felt the shame of being a prostitute, selling myself for sex. I felt that I made that choice so I felt so much shame and guilt because I felt that I was dirty, nasty, disgusting, worthless and unlovable. I was lower than dirt! Who does that? I felt the shame and guilt of being treated the way I was by my father. What had I done to make him hate me so much? Was I so horrible that my own father couldn't love me? It wasn't until I started my healing process that I realized that it wasn't my fault! It wasn't me that had the issue. I wasn't the one exploiting women; I was the one being exploited. I was the one being victimized! And as far as my father was concerned, he was the adult and I was the child. I only wanted to make my father happy and proud of me.

It wasn't my fault that he had an anger issue and when anything went wrong I was his punching bag or when he would drink he would rape me. It wasn't my fault that he did the same thing to a couple of my friends as well, but I held on to that shame and guilt. It was not mine to hold on to, it belonged to him. The shame and guilt should have been on my abusers and traffickers, not me.

So hear me when I say this!

IT WAS NOT YOUR FAULT!

Let go of the shame! Let go of the guilt!

It's not yours to hold on to!

Self-Check

What do you think of when you think of freedom?

_____

_____

_____

_____

_____

_____

How important is freedom in YOUR life?

_____

_____

_____

_____

There are so many "things" that can keep us bound such as resentment, anger, guilt, and shame, just to name a few.

135

What keeps you bound? Have you kept these things hidden?

_____

_____

_____

_____

_____

What shame and guilt are you holding on to?

_____

_____

_____

_____

_____

The longer you keep these bondages in the dark, the longer you stay bound. Until you shine a light on your bondage you can't heal.

Below are some scriptures that you can study to see what God's Word has to say about freedom and bondage.

2 Corinthians 3:17 ESV - Now the Lord is the Spirit, and where the Spirit of the Lord is, there is freedom.

Galatians 5:1 ESV - For freedom Christ has set us free; stand firm therefore, and do not submit again to a yoke of slavery.

Luke 4:18-19 ESV

"The Spirit of the Lord is upon me, because he has anointed me to proclaim good news to the poor. He has sent me to proclaim liberty to the captives and recovering of sight to the blind, to set at liberty those who are oppressed, to proclaim the year of the Lord's favour."

Webster's dictionary defines grace as:
1 a : unmerited divine assistance given humans for their regeneration or sanctification
* b : a virtue coming from God*
* c : a state of sanctification enjoyed through divine grace*
2 a : approval, favor <stayed in his good graces>
* b archaic : mercy, pardon*
c : a special favor : privilege <each in his place, by right, not grace, shall rule his heritage — Rudyard Kipling>
d : disposition to or an act or instance of kindness, courtesy, or clemency
e : a temporary exemption : reprieve

2 Corinthians 12:9 ESV

But he said to me, "My grace is sufficient for you, for my power is made perfect in weakness." Therefore, I will boast all the more gladly of my weaknesses, so that the power of Christ may rest upon me.

Ephesians 2:8-9 ESV

For by grace you have been saved through faith. And this is not your own doing; it is the gift of God, not a result of works, so that no one may boast.

WHO AM I

How many times has someone "labelled" you? How many times have you labelled someone else? Have you judged someone before you even knew anything about them? I remember growing up my father telling me I was worthless and would never amount to anything. He labelled me as a slut and continuously accused me of sleeping with a lot of men when that wasn't the case at all. The traffickers that I had been with labelled me as a piece of property to be sold in order for them to make a profit. The purchasers or "tricks" labelled me as a sex toy that they could do anything with. My abusers labelled me as worthless and as someone they could use and *treated me with total disregard for my humanity and best interests*. Are you getting the picture here?

I have heard it told time and time again that words are powerful. God's word says that "life and death are in the tongue" Proverbs 18:21. The words someone else speaks or even what we say about who we are can be very powerful over how our lives turn out. If we are constantly negative, our lives will be negative. I can't tell you how many times I heard growing up that I "was nothing and would never be anything" and the sad part about that is that I believed it and so my life turned to a downward spiral. I never thought I was worth anything good and I honestly believed I was a horrible person.

There are many times when labels are very hurtful. We never want to be labelled something ugly or something that just isn't truly who we are. How does it make you feel when you're being labelled? In all actuality when we are being labelled, the individual labelling us, is making judgements or assumptions about how we are and who we can be. Labels are others people's opinion and can often limit or hurt. *What labels have been put on you? I know the labels put on me were shameful, dirty, nasty, horrifying and all hurtful and untrue.* To heal it is important to turn those labels into positives so they work for you instead of against you. I know for me once I started my healing process I made a list of the words and labels that I heard, often shouted in an angry rage, that left my heart in pieces and shaped my image of me. For instance, I was told that I was nothing and I would never be anything I had to turn that around and say I am somebody, I am worthy, I will do something, and finally I am doing something with my life. All those negative words and labels programmed our mind and heart to believe and act as if they were true. To take back our lives and god given gifts and talents we need to reprogram our minds and hearts, to the truth of who God say's we are. Remember you did not develop the negative thoughts and beliefs about you over night and you will not replace them with truth without time and work. It's important to be gentle with yourself. I hope you take the opportunity to do the work that I have listed below answer these questions honestly and truly. Be sure that you take some quiet time during the self-check and really dig deep to find out what it was that was said to you how were you labelled and turn it around and make it for your good. Invite Jesus to speak directly to your heart, and ask him to show you his truth, about the words and labels that you now carry as wounds. He meets us each differently and often differently moment by moment, based on what we need. He may put a thought in your head, show you an image causing you to remember or feel something. Be willing to sit and allow his truth to heal the hurt, he does not play hide and seek with those who are crying out from their heart.

What labels are you putting on yourself? It's important to be careful about the words you speak about yourself. Remember you can abuse you as easily and terribly as others. Don't allow what people have said about you in the past to determine who you are. We heard such negative things, for so long, that the lies spoken to us become our beliefs about our worth, value and potential. Once we believe them our abusers control our thoughts and no longer need to control us physically; because we have accepted their perspective about us. It is time to start loving ourselves and realizing who we truly are. You are worth so much more than what people have told you. You are beautiful, you are smart, you can do anything you set your mind to do, you are worthy, you are love, you are special, and you are unique. So walk in your uniqueness because there is only one you and you are amazing!

SELF-CHECK

What were some of the negative words that you have heard
that shaped your life in a negative way?

_____

_____

_____

_____

_____

_____

How did you feel when you heard these words?

_____

_____

_____

_____

_____

_____

Did this have a negative effect on how you saw/see yourself?
Do you still think negatively about yourself?

_____

_____

_____

_____

_____

_____

How do you think God sees you? And why do you feel this

way?

_____

_____

_____

_____

_____

_____

_____

_____

For every negative word that you have heard about you (listed above) get into Gods word and find what God says about you!

_____

_____

_____

_____

_____

_____

_____

Below are some scriptures of what God has to say about you. If need be, write these scriptures on index cards and place them where you can see them. Use the scriptures as a reminder of what God thinks of you and not what man thinks of you.

Psalm 139:14 - I praise you, for I am fearfully and wonderfully made. Wonderful are your works; my soul knows it very well.

Luke 12:7 - Indeed, the very hairs of your head are all numbered. Don't be afraid; you are worth more than many sparrows.

Redemption

As I sit here thinking about redemption I really felt the need that it's important to spend some time to look at redemption. When we are struggling to see clearly through our shame it's difficult to understand a concept like redemption. We know what the word means in our head BUT do we really know it in our heart? Can we really dare draw close to our redemption when our shame and secrets are bigger than our love of self? We have been through so much in our lives and often survived by learning to please other people that we think that's the way we have to be with Jesus! His death on the cross and resurrection already paid the price for our sin! We have been redeemed with a price...it's a free gift! We can't do ANYTHING to earn that redemption! If redemption could be earned God would not have endured such a horrible death to pay our price.

Have you ever lied (even a little white lie), cheated (maybe on a test at school), stole (even a piece of candy), acted jealously (with a boyfriend or husband), was envious (wanted something someone else has), got drunk, been selfish, been greedy (even with food), etc.? I think you get the point! I have had people tell me, "Kelley, you don't understand, I lived such a life of disgust! I am a horrible person!" I have even heard, "Well I haven't really done anything wrong. Nothing that nobody else hasn't done! I'm a really good person!" And here's the thing.... SIN IS SIN!!! Period...end of story! There is no sin greater than any other sin! From the sweet little old lady that tells just a "little white lie" to her husband to a gang member that murders someone, it's the same in Gods eyes and they both need redemption! And the beauty of it is that God loves us all the same!!! Acts 10:34 says, "Then Peter began to speak: Now I realize how true it is that God does not show favouritism." WE CAN ALL BE REDEEMED!

As a child I was not raised up in church but my grandmother attended a Roman Catholic Church. So as a child if I did anything wrong she would tell me that I was going to hell and there was nothing that I can do to redeem myself. So I lived my life as if there was no hope for me. As I grew older and I was invited to church I actually believe that if I ever walked into a church the church would blow up, because of all the bad things I had done, seen and been through. I didn't think that I was redeemable and I had a lot of people in my life that agreed. I knew nothing about Jesus and his love for me. Thankfully Jesus and a few others, like those dope boys who refused to sell to me, saw the good in me. I never understood what Jesus' death on the cross truly meant, but when I was ready to do the work of healing I was drawn to him. It took years of going to Church and getting into the Bible to actually believe in my heart that I was redeemable.

When I didn't or couldn't believe that anyone would pay the price for my mess up's and then want to give me the gift of redemption I walked with my head down. My heart did not "feel" worthy of redemption. I would watch people in the church and think to myself I know they think they're better than me **AND** I know I don't belong here. I thought that God could not love me because of all the bad things I had done. When I married my forever husband I felt the same way about him. I was convinced that he believed that he was better than me. I now recognize that this belief came from my deep feelings of inadequacy. I felt unworthy of his love. Sadly, I didn't know how to deal with the hurt, both real and perceived and so it kept me away from God and his redeeming love. In my mind I felt that if the people in the church we're going to hurt me than God was likely to do the same. What I didn't realize was that the church is like a hospital for the sick. There is no one including the pastor of any church that is perfect and that doesn't need redemption. We all have things that we need grace mercy and redemption for. We all need God's read deeming love. We can't earn it, we have to believe in our hearts and have that faith that God has redeemed us. And every one is worthy of God's love and redemption.

Webster's (Merriam-Webster Dictionary, n.d.) **dictionary defines "REDEEM" as:**

1 a: to buy back: repurchase b: to get or win back
2: to free from what distresses or harms: as a: to free from captivity by payment of ransom b: to extricate from or help to overcome something detrimental c: to release from blame or

debt: clear d: to free from the consequences of sin

3: to change for the better: reform

4: repair, restore

5 a: to free from a lien by payment of an amount secured thereby b (1): to remove the obligation of by payment <the United States Treasury redeems savings bonds on demand> (2): to exchange for something of value <redeem trading stamps> c: to make good:

6 a: to atone for: expiate <redeem an error> b (1): to offset the bad effect of (2): to make worthwhile:

So we know what the definition of redeem is but do we really know why we need redemption? Romans 3:23 says, "For we have ALL sinned and fallen short of the glory of God," So in that case if we have all sinned then we ALL need redemption! So what is sin?

Webster's (Merriam-Webster Dictionary, n.d.) **dictionary defines sin as:**

1 a: an offense against religious or moral law b: an action that is or is felt to be highly reprehensible <it's a sin to waste food> c: an often serious shortcoming: fault

2 a: transgression of the law of God b: a vitiated state of human nature in which the self is estranged from God

Now let's see what the bible says about sin:

James 4:17 ESV - So whoever knows the right thing to do and fails to do it, for him it is sin.

1 John 1:8-10 ESV - If we say we have no sin, we deceive ourselves, and the truth is not in us. If we confess our sins, he is faithful and just to forgive us our sins and to cleanse us from all unrighteousness. If we say we have not sinned, we make him a liar, and his word is not in us.

1 John 3:4 ESV - Everyone who makes a practice of sinning also practices lawlessness; sin is lawlessness.

John 8:34 ESV - Jesus answered them, "Truly, truly, I say to you, everyone who commits sin is a slave to sin.

Romans 6:23 ESV - For the wages of sin is death, but the free gift of God is eternal life in Christ Jesus our Lord. And he really got specific when he listed sin in this scripture:

Galatians 5:19-21 ESV - Now the works of the flesh are evident: sexual immorality, impurity, sensuality, idolatry, sorcery, enmity, strife, jealousy, fits of anger, rivalries, dissensions, divisions, envy, drunkenness, orgies, and things like these. I warn you, as I warned you before, that those who do such things will not inherit the kingdom of God.

Study Romans 8: my suggestion would be to read it in different versions such as NIV, NLT, Message and Amplified. (There are many Bible apps that can help you with this so you aren't purchasing multiple bibles.) There are so many nuggets in this particular chapter.

What verse(s) stood out to you the most and why?

_____

_____

_____

_____

_____

_____

_____

_____

_____

_____

_____

_____

_____

_____

_____

_____

What did you get out of this chapter?

_____

_____

_____

_____

_____

_____

_____

_____

_____

_____

_____

_____

_____

_____

_____

_____

Here are some of the things that I found to really help me in this chapter:

1.   We are no longer condemned (vs.1)

2.   We have been set free from the law of sin and death (vs.2)

3.   We are righteous (vs. 10)

4.   We have been "adopted" by God (vs. 15-16)

5.   We are co-heirs with Christ (vs. 17)

6.   The Holy Spirit helps us when we are weak. (vs. 26)

7.   We have been called, justified & glorified by God for his purpose (vs. 28-30)

8.   God justifies us (vs. 31-34)

9.   We are more than conquerors (vs. 37)

10.   NOONE can separate us from the love of God (vs. 38-39)

How will these "truths" help you in your walk?

_____

_____

_____

_____

_____

_____

A Beautiful You

Have you ever met someone that you immediately thought "WOW, she is beautiful"? She seemed to have the perfect figure, the perfect facial features, the perfect hair, the perfect skin, perfect smile and even her clothing was perfect!!! BUT THEN.....she opened her mouth to speak and WHOA.....what a mouth! She was rude, mean, and everything that came out of her mouth was negative! What's your first thought after that? I know for me it's usually, "She is just horrible"! But then on the flip side, have you ever met someone that maybe was just "average" in the world's eyes? Maybe she had a few extra pounds, hair was just thrown up in a ponytail, very casual looking and maybe not even the most perfect teeth but after leaving her presence you thought, "WOW! She is absolutely beautiful"! While you were around her you felt uplifted and happy. Now that's the kind of beauty I want to be around. That's how I would rather people view me as "beautiful"! I guess the older I have gotten the more important it is for people to view my insides more than my outsides but I didn't always feel that way.

A diamond is full of worth and value – a thing of beauty to be treasured. It sparkles and shines and it stands out. A beautiful piece of artwork and every diamond is unique. The

154

diamond is too precious to let go of. Diamonds are also one of the strongest materials. But before the diamond became a thing of beauty and worth it had to endure stress. Not only does the formation require stress but extreme amounts of heat as well. So just as the diamond requires stress and extreme amount of heat in our lives we will endure stress adversity and the heat will rise but that is what's going to shape us into the beautiful diamond that we the will become. We are all diamonds in the rough.

True beauty comes from the inside. We have to allow our beauty from the inside to shine out. What do people see when you walk in the room? Are you allowing your true beauty from within shine or are you just showing up as a dressed up mess? We can always dress up the outside but that won't do us any good if our inside is toxic.

Webster's (Merriam-Webster Dictionary, n.d.) dictionary defines Beauty as:

1: the quality or aggregate of qualities in a person or thing that gives pleasure to the senses or pleasurably exalts the mind or spirit:

2: a beautiful person or thing; especially: a beautiful woman

3: a particularly graceful, ornamental, or excellent quality

1 Peter 3:3-4 - Do not let your adorning be external — the braiding of hair and the putting on of gold jewellery, or the clothing you wear — but let your adorning be the hidden person of the heart with the imperishable beauty of a gentle and quiet spirit, which in God's sight is very precious.

1 Samuel 16:7 - But the Lord said to Samuel, "Do not look on his appearance or on the height of his stature, because I have rejected him. For the Lord sees not as man sees: man looks on the outward appearance, but the Lord looks on the heart."

When you look in the mirror what do you see? Do you like what you see? Do you see a work of art created by God? Do you see all of your flaws and imperfections? What is your INITIAL thought? Do you even look in the mirror or do you avoid them? What do you think God sees? Do you think God makes mistakes? Do you think he creates junk?

Describe to me what YOU think God was thinking when he made you.

_____

_____

_____

_____

_____

_____

_____

Why do you feel this way?

_____

_____

_____

_____

_____

_____

Does Gods word line up with why you feel that way? If so,
find the scripture to back it up.

_____

_____

_____

_____

_____

_____

Our thought process can largely affect how we think of ourselves. If we can change our minds we can change our negative attitudes and thoughts about ourselves. I have to wake up every morning and on purpose look in the mirror and tell myself, "God loves YOU!!! You are special!! You are more than a conqueror! You can do ALL things through Christ that strengthens you!" For so many years all I heard were negative words but those that "loved" me. I heard things such as "You are nothing and will never be anything", "Your fat", "and you're ugly" and some very derogatory words that no woman should ever be called. After hearing these words for so long I believed them. So now I have to take 40+ years of negativity and Re-program my mind by feeding it with positive words.

What words or phrases did you hear that were programmed in your mind about yourself?

_____

_____

_____

_____

_____

_____

_____

What words or phrases do you need to replace them with?

_____

_____

_____

_____

_____

Make a commitment for at least one month to look in the mirror EVERYDAY and tell yourself the positive, good and holy things that YOU ARE!!! Look up scriptures about who God says you are and say them our loud every day!!! Remember: You ARE special! You ARE loved! You ARE more than a conqueror!

YOU ARE BEAUTIFUL AND A TREASURE TO GOD!!!!

Forgiveness

God's Forgiveness, forgiving others and forgiving ourselves. These are such important topics!

Webster's (Merriam-Webster Dictionary, n.d.) **dictionary defines "Forgive" as**
: to stop feeling anger toward (someone who has done something wrong) : to stop blaming (someone)
: to stop feeling anger about (something) : to forgive someone for (something wrong)

How many of us are really forgiving, as we should? Are we receiving God's forgiveness? Or are we constantly asking God to forgive us over and over again for something he has already forgiven us for and forgotten!! How many of us have forgiven ourselves? Yes, I said forgive ourselves!! All of these things are so important for our healing process. We will take each one of these 3 areas of forgiveness and get a real understanding of how important it is for us to receive God's forgiveness, forgive others and forgive ourselves.

GOD'S FORGIVENESS

Before we look at the other 2 areas of forgiveness we will see what God's word has to say about HIS forgiveness of our sins.

1 John 1:9 ESV - If we confess our sins, he is faithful and just to forgive us our sins and to cleanse us from all unrighteousness.

Romans 3:23-26 ESV - For all have sinned and fall short of the glory of God, and are justified by his grace as a gift, through the redemption that is in Christ Jesus, whom God put forward as a propitiation by his blood, to be received by faith. This was to show God's righteousness, because in his divine forbearance he had passed over former sins. It was to show his righteousness at the present time, so that he might be just and the justifier of the one who has faith in Jesus.

2 Chronicles 7:14 - If my people who are called by my name humble themselves, and pray and seek my face and turn from their wicked ways, then I will hear from heaven and will forgive their sin and heal their land.

These are just a few scriptures that talk about God's forgiveness of our sin. God loves us and wants each and every one of us in right standing with him. So now I have a question for you.....

Do you believe that God has forgiven you of all your sin? I don't mean believing in your mind but what about from your heart. Why or why not?

_____

_____

_____

_____

_____

_____

Do you realize that once we confess our sin and ask God to forgive us he also forgets them!!! We are the ones that keep reminding him!! It is so important that we also receive his forgiveness. God is not like man that has conditions on forgiveness.

Isaiah 43:25 ESV - "I, I am he who blots out your transgressions for my own sake, and I will not remember your sins."

Hebrews 8:12 ESV - "For I will be merciful toward their iniquities, and I will remember their sins no more."

Psalm 103:12 ESV - As far as the east is from the west, so far does he remove our transgressions from us.

Hebrews 10:17 ESV - Then he adds, "I will remember their sins and their lawless deeds no more."

All of the above scriptures should bring you comfort in knowing that not only does God forgive but he also forgets our sin!!!

We have talked about God's forgiveness for us but what about us forgiving others? Yes, we are to forgive others!!! Yes, even the ones that abused us, used us, talked about us, hurt us! I know, you may be thinking, "Kelley, you have surely lost your mind! I am not going to forgive _____! You have no idea what they did to me!"

Well, let's see what God's word has to say about forgiving others.

Ephesians 4:32 ESV - Be kind to one another, tender-hearted, forgiving one another, as God in Christ forgave you.

Mark 11:25 ESV - And whenever you stand praying, forgive, if you have anything against anyone, so that your Father also who is in heaven may forgive you your trespasses."

Luke 17:3-4 ESV - Pay attention to yourselves! If your brother sins, rebuke him, and if he repents, forgive him, and if he sins against you seven times in the day, and turns to you seven times, saying, 'I repent,' you must forgive him."

Matthew 6:14 ESV - For if you forgive others their trespasses, your heavenly Father will also forgive you,

Luke 6:37 ESV - "Judge not, and you will not be judged; condemn not, and you will not be condemned; forgive, and you will be forgiven;

Colossians 3:13 ESV - Bearing with one another and, if one has a complaint against another, forgiving each other; as the Lord has forgiven you, so you also must forgive.

As I read the above scriptures, we are to forgive EVERYBODY! Colossians 3:13 even says, "as the Lord has forgiven you, so you MUST forgive." Now I have to admit when I first started studying forgiveness I was not happy to see these scriptures. I was not ready to forgive, the hurt felt too big and too raw. I was even at times angry and confused that God would ask me to forgive people who did such unspeakable and life altering things to me. BUT, that is exactly what he was and is asking us all to do. I would think to myself why should I forgive those that hurt me so deeply. I couldn't understand how God could want me to forgive them. That included my dad who raped me, abused me physically, mentally & emotionally, all the abusive exes, the pimps who sold me and tortured me, those that have talked bad about me, hurt my feelings and so on! Trust me I had a **HUGE** list of folks that I needed to forgive. Some of them took longer than others for me to forgive. I started the process of forgiveness with a heart that was literally pained just thinking about forgiving the worst offenses. I did not want to forgive. I was still angry and confused about why God requires we forgive. I wanted to stay mad and keep score of all the things people had done to me. The list of what they did was much longer than the list of what I did, or at least that's what I told myself. People who molest children and sell humans don't deserve forgiveness. At the same time, I wanted no needed the peace of knowing I was forgiven by God. I knew enough to understand that forgiveness is a big deal to Jesus and that I didn't really understand His kind of forgiveness. I wondered did I actually have to go to them and say I forgive you? Did it count as forgiveness just by saying it or did I have to mean it and if I had to mean it how was my heart ever going to get there? It took a long, long time. I didn't forgive everyone or every offense at the same time. I started just by saying "Ok Jesus I know this is important and you know I don't really want to forgive them; so I guess I need your help to change my heart and help me want to forgive."

I asked for help so many times I was beginning to think I really might never be able to forgive for real. Over time I noticed my heart did change, as my understanding of forgiveness grew. I thought that forgiving them would be like me saying it was ok or that the things they did to me didn't matter. Except it did matter! As I got to know God more I began to understand that my hurt matters a lot to me but matters so much more to God. Forgiveness does not dismiss or minimize my pain or their wrongs. Actually, by forgiving I was saying **"God my heart hurts so much because of the wrongs and violations other people did to me. Yet, I can see that really there is nothing I could ever do to them and nothing they could give me or say that would restore me."** No person can ever undo the knowledge I have of being raped instead of nurtured and protected by my dad. There is no sentence my traffickers could be given that

166

would undo the impact of thousands of rapes, on my body and heart. God's standard and definition of forgiveness is not ours. When I forgave I was saying **"God I release my rights to hold a grudge or take vengeance to you. There is no judgment t I can hand out that would be right, or begin to repay me, so I am giving my rights for vengeance over to you, because only you can give me justice and make me whole."**

Every time the topic of forgiveness came up I cringed but I kept asking God to change my heart and help me understand. I asked for the wisdom and the strength to actually have forgiveness in my heart, over and over, until I began authentically forgiving the smaller "offenses". In time, with a lot of work, and a lot of learning what forgiveness is and is not I step by step was able to forgive even the biggest offenses. I learned that forgiveness is not about the people who hurt us, it's for us. When we hold grudges and cling to our claim for pay back we keep our already hurting heart tightly connected to the people who hurt us. We empower our abusers along with all those people who just treated us meanly to control our emotions and out healing. They do not deserve that power! **Refusing to forgive does not help us, it doesn't validate our pain, undo the hurt, make what happened more real or matter more, it doesn't restore or even make the person who hurt us in any way uncomfortable**. In truth it accomplishes nothing except holds us in pain and connected to trauma instead of allowing us to heal and step free from captivity. Remember earlier when I explained that God views all sin as equal? From his perspective all un-forgiven sin, from the "innocent" white lie to serial killers leads to the same eternal separation and destruction. Obviously, the consequences here are and should be different between a white lie and murder, but eternally God is holy and just and he will not tolerate sin. He loves every person that does not mean he approves or likes the choices we make, but he nonetheless loves us all. His desire and plan is for everyone to accept His offer of redemption, but we get to pick whether or not we do.

Forgiveness matters to God not only because of the pain un-forgiveness adds to our heart, but because he paid a heavy price for our redemption. If God, who gave up his life for our redemption chose to forgive me of everything I have done, then really who do I think I am by refusing to forgive people, who God loves and died for.

As a young Christian first realizing that God is serious about forgiveness I feared I would have to go to each person who hurt me and forgive them, face to face. For those who have come out of abusive and dysfunctional relationships that could have some real risk. God does not expect us to put ourselves at risk or to even expose us to people who hurt us and have not changed. Forgiveness is an internal heart choice, where we simply release our claims and rights for justice and vengeance to God who is SO much better equipped to actually give us the justice our hearts need. There are still times my heart goes through this back-and-forth tug of war on whether I can forgive. I have learned that most of the time this is my hearts way to letting me know there is a new, deeper layer of hurt that needs my attention. As we are able to be obedient to God's word we receive a beautiful gift in exchange.

FREEDOM!!!! Yes, I said freedom. There are many things that are attached to un-forgiveness such as anger, rage, bitterness, and resentment. These things hinder our healing process and keep us in the "victim" mentality and keep us in bondage. While we are angry, hurt, resentful, etc. the person we are angry at doesn't have a clue and living their life carefree!!! Meanwhile we are miserable. That is not what God intends for us. Jesus died to give us life and live it to the full! How can we live in freedom when we are bound by un-forgiveness and all that it brings?

Matthew 5:43-45 (NKJV) - You have heard that is was said, 'You shall love your neighbour and hate your enemy'. But I say to you, love your enemies, bless those who curse you, do good to those who hate you, and pray for those who spitefully use you and persecute you, that you may be sons of your Father in heaven; for He makes His sun rise on the evil and on the good, and sends rain on the just and on the unjust.

Write a list of those that you have not forgiven:

_____

_____

_____

_____

_____

_____

_____

_____

_____

_____

_____

I have been asked several times, "So does forgiving this person or people mean I need to keep them in my life if they have abused me?"

If there is someone that has hurt you who is toxic (verbally, mentally, physically, emotionally or sexually abusive, negative, ungodly, etc.) then no you don't have to have them in your life! Just because you make the choice to forgive that doesn't mean that they have free reign to treat you like a doormat. God would never want you to be in harm's way. Get the toxic folks out of your life especially if you are trying to live a godly life. You may even have to distance yourself or let go of family members for some time while you are healing. Ask God to help you through the letting go process. There are many times that "family" is our worst critics. Be sure to have people in your inner circle that are Godly and POSITIVE!!!

Matthew 6:14-15 (NKJV) - For if you forgive men their trespasses, your heavenly Father will also forgive you. But if you do not forgive men their trespasses, neither will your Father forgive your trespasses.

Forgiveness is the key to freedom.
Forgiveness is freedom from angry or resentful feelings.
Forgiveness is releasing an offense, difference or mistake.
Forgiveness is ceasing to demand punishment or restitution.
Forgiveness is a choice.
Forgiveness is by faith and in obedience.
Forgiveness is commanded in the Bible.

So now that we have talked about God's forgiveness and forgiving others I have a question for you. Have you forgiven yourself? Yes, I said have you forgiven yourself? How much harm have we done, not only to others but also to ourselves? A huge part of forgiveness is the ability to forgive us! We are human and make mistakes but we must stop dwelling on those mistakes? We aren't supposed to judge others but we must also not judge ourselves too harshly either! Do an inventory on our character and ourselves so we can change, yes! We are not GOD! How many times have you said to yourself, "I really wish I hadn't done _____ or _____."? How often do you beat yourself up for choices or mistakes that you may have made? Maybe something you said something or did something that hurt someone else or even you. I can't tell you how many times satan has used my past mistakes and choices as a way for me to torture myself.

I would tell myself over and over again how horrible I was and what a piece of garbage I was and I really would tear myself down! Well, isn't that a form of abuse? When we talk negatively about ourselves we don't hurt anyone else but us! Do you think God wants that? If God forgives and forgets then why can't we? God loves us and considers us his precious children. He doesn't want us hurting ourselves because in turn it hurts Him! Consider this, what if your child made a mistake and you corrected and forgave your child but he/she couldn't and wouldn't forgive themselves. How would that make you feel? You would hurt for your child wouldn't you? Well, how much more do you think God feels about it when we do that same thing? God loves us more than we could ever imagine and if we hurt....he hurts. We have been freed from our sins and there is no condemnation!!

I wanted to do a search on what the bible had to say about this and I really like the way this was worded: "Never does the Bible talk about the idea of "forgiving yourself." We are told to forgive others when they trespass against us and seek forgiveness. When we ask for God's forgiveness based upon Christ having already paid for our sins and our having trusted in Him as Saviour and Lord, He forgives us. It is as simple as that (1 John 1:9). However, even though we are released from the bondage to sin (as spoken of in Romans chapters 6-8), we can still choose to wallow in it and act as though we are not freed from it. Likewise, with guilty feelings, we can accept the fact that we are forgiven in Christ, or we can believe the devil's lie that we are still guilty and should therefore feel guilty." (Got Questions Ministries, n.d.)

Here are some of the effects of not forgiving yourself: Feelings of guilt

- Shame

- Depression

- Self-hatred

- Self-loathing

- Low/no self-esteem

- Relational issues

Self-Check

What are you not letting go of? Once you make this list be sure to go to God in prayer and ask him to help you to forgive yourself and let go of the former sin.

_____

_____

_____

_____

_____

_____

_____

_____

_____

_____

_____

_____

_____

_____

So we have talked about God's forgiveness, forgiving others and forgiving ourselves so now what? This next exercise may be difficult but it is really needed in order to move forward and bring freedom and healing. And remember, this is for you not the person you are forgiving. You will need your list of those that you still haven't forgiven for this.

Repeat this out loud:

"Lord, I release _____ to you. I choose to forgive them in the name of Jesus! I tear down and destroy the spirit of abuse behind these people, in Jesus' name. I speak salvation into their lives." Amen.

After you have prayed the above prayer jot down some notes below on what happened when you chose to forgive and release these people. How are you feeling? Is there anyone you should have added but didn't? Are you willing to start by just asking God to help your heart understand why you are struggling to forgive and to bring you the understanding and healing you need to be free from the places this person holds your heart captive? Commit to pray for your heart and those individuals, you forgave and those you couldn't, for the next 30 days. The changes may surprise you. Your first few days may be quick, short, begrudging prayers but as the days pass you may feel God softening your heart and you will see yourself praying more earnest, heartfelt prayers for them. This is not to say that you have to have them in your life but what does happen as you pray for them is you will feel a true release in your heart from the hurts they have done to you.

Here's what God's word says about praying for those that hurt you:

Matthew 5:44 ESV - But I say to you, Love your enemies and pray for those who persecute you,

Luke 6:27-28 ESV - "But I say to you who hear, Love your enemies, do good to those who hate you, bless those who curse you, pray for those who abuse you.

After saying that prayer and releasing those that have hurt you, how did that make you feel?

_____

_____

_____

_____

_____

_____

_____

LOVE

Normally when people hear the word love they automatically think male/female relationships but there is so much more to love than sex. Love for God, Love for our children, love for others, love for "things", and the often forgotten yet critically important love for ourselves. How can we truly love others when we don't love ourselves? Self-hatred, low self-esteem, low self-worth is dangerous for us. In this chapter we will dig into the word and see what God says about loving ourselves and love in general. A balanced perspective around loving ourselves is healthy for us as well as everyone around us.

When I did a Google search for "Definition of Love" there were 341 million results.

Webster's (Merriam-Webster Dictionary, n.d.) **Dictionary defines love as:**
(1): strong affection for another arising out of kinship or personal ties <maternal love for a child> (2): attraction based on sexual desire: affection and tenderness felt by lovers (3): affection based on admiration, benevolence, or common interests <love for his old schoolmates>

When I did a Google search for "Gods definition of Love" there were 21 million results.

The Greek language (the language of the New Testament) uses two different words to describe and define love. The most commonly used Greek word translated "love" in the New Testament is "agape". This love is represented by God's love for us. It is a non-partial, sacrificial love probably best exemplified by God's provision for our rebellion:

John 3:16 ESV - "For God so loved (agape) the world, that he gave his only Son, that whoever believes in him should not perish but have eternal life.

The gift of God's son as a provision for sin was given to all humans, regardless of who we are. God's free gift of redemption for us flows from His unconditional love for us.

In our humanity we often tend to love conditionally, based on what we want and need or in reaction to how we are treated. This kind of love is based upon the familiarity and direct interaction. The Greek word "phileo" defines this kind of love, often translated "brotherly love". Phileo is soulish (connected through our emotions) kind of love in contrast to agape, which is love extended through the spirit. Agape love requires a relationship with God through Jesus Christ, since the non-regenerated soul is unable to love unconditionally. Agape love gives and sacrifices expecting nothing back in return.

1 John 4:8 ESV - Anyone who does not love does not know God, because God is love.

1 Corinthians 13:4-7 ESV - Love is patient and kind; love does not envy or boast; it is not arrogant or rude. It does not insist on its own way; it is not irritable or resentful; it does not rejoice at wrongdoing, but rejoices with the truth. Love bears all things, believes all things, hopes all things, and endures all things.

There are so many people that don't truly love themselves. If people actually loved themselves, they would not put themselves down they would not have low self-esteem they would not try to harm themselves they would not try to stay and unhealthy relationships and the list goes on and on. What are you doing for self-love? Do you take the time to truly show yourself love? You may be asking yourself Kelley what in the world are you talking about? What I'm talking about is that self-care taking care of self. What are you doing to be good to yourself? What are you doing to show yourself that you are worthy of love from yourself and others? What are you doing to take care of you? Yes, it is good to do the inside work and the healing process but what about taking care of your hair your nails your skin your clothes how you look how you present yourself? Taking care of ourselves makes a statement to our own hearts and to others. I get it as a woman, in general and especially for those of us healing from abuse, it is easy to get distracted by taking care of everyone else first. I know, for me, this was because I was always trying to make up for being bad or to earn a place at the good enough table. I had to work to understand that God does not want or need anything from me in exchange. I had no example that was agape love from people, when I got saved, to pull from as a reference. I learned yes by reading his word but so much more by focusing on letting him build our relationship – I didn't know how. Experiencing his unconditional love that did not run, change or even get mad at me for blowing it over and over is what helped me learn to love others and myself. We are to love others as He loves us. Until we step fully into a relationship with God, and learn to love in healthy safe ways we can't comprehend loving or being loved without putting personal agenda first.

However, once we are looking at our life and worth, separated from our shame, our desire and emotional capacity change and, often for the first time, we can believe that it's possible for God to love us unconditionally. His love doesn't have exceptions or strings. He loves us moment by moment where we am. His love cannot be earned, so my effort to earn it was a waste of time. But if we don't take care of ourselves how can we take care of anyone else? And it all starts with self-love.

Let me give you an example of what I mean. There are times that I just want to sit back and read a book or watch a movie on the Hallmark Channel. Sometimes I just needed quiet time alone in my head with Jesus, sometimes I wanted to go to the movies by myself. I like to do something special whenever I have accomplished something that is a big deal to my heart and it's important to me that those moments be celebrated without feeling like I need to explain or justify, so often these are also times I allow myself to step away. In the past I would have wanted "me" time but dismissed my real need as irrelevant because everyone else's needs and wants came first and were always bigger than mine. As I learned what love is I was slowly able to see that putting me first was not only sometimes ok, but it's actually a healthy and wise new habit. I am not talking about becoming self-absorbed or over indulged in me. I am talking about recognizing and caring for my soul needs. ***And you know what it's okay, healthy and important to do that!***

That's part of self-care. I don't always have to be doing something for someone else and not think about myself, because doing so leaves me exhausted, run down and feeling once again insignificant.

SELF-CHECK

Do you love yourself? Why or Why not?

_____

_____

_____

_____

_____

_____

_____

Do you believe that God loves you? Why or Why not?

_____

_____

_____

_____

_____

_____

_____

Do you think Gods love is conditional? Why or why not?

_____

_____

_____

_____

_____

_____

_____

_____

Here are some scriptures that show Gods love for us:

1 John 4:10 ESV - In this is love, not that we have loved God but that he loved us and sent his Son to be the propitiation for our sins.

1 John 4:19 ESV - We love because he first loved us.

Romans 8:35-39 ESV - Who shall separate us from the love of Christ? Shall tribulation, or distress, or persecution, or famine, or nakedness, or danger, or sword? As it is written, "For your sake we are being killed all the day long; we are regarded as sheep to be slaughtered." No, in all these things we are more than conquerors through him who loved us. For I am sure that neither death nor life, nor angels nor rulers, nor things present nor things to come, nor powers, nor height nor depth, nor anything else in all creation, will be able to separate us from the love of God in Christ Jesus our Lord.

Romans 5:8 ESV - But God shows his love for us in that while we were still sinners, Christ died for us. Do you think it hurts God when we don't love ourselves? If God loves, we should love ourselves! No matter what anyone has said or done to us we need to know how special we are in Gods eyes!!!

The "Fathers" Love

In this chapter we will discuss a father's love as well as THE Fathers love. For a young girl, a father's love is extremely important but sadly for a lot of us we didn't get that or if we did it was a twisted form of abuse labeled as love. Abuse leaves life-long scars, regardless of whether it's physical, emotional, verbal and even sexual abuse. When the perpetrator is a parent or primary caretaker the destruction on our beliefs, capacity to trust, relationships, perception of self and God, and on our emotions impacts every aspect of our life. These warped perspectives can change our lives in such a negative way. It can affect the men we pick, how we see ourselves, how we think, talk and act. BUT we have a father in heaven that can heal and change our warped perspectives and that's what we will see in this Chapter. So get ready to dig into Gods word and let the healing begin!

Now I have to say that accepting God as my father was a real struggle. I kept hearing that if your earthly father loves you and does good things for you then how much more will your heavenly father do for you. For years I cringed every time I heard that. I thought about all of the things that my father had done to me and could only conclude from the verse that God was going to hurt me – It was just a matter of time. As a kid I always heard that God was going to punish me and so I came into the relationship with Jesus holding onto to big fears of God's "inevitable" punishment. My father had been predictably abusive and intentionally tearing down. As a little girl he was the monster in my nightmares. As a teen and your adult men continued to demonstrate that they should be feared and that, generally speaking, men didn't regard my humanity as even worth consideration. I know there are many women that feel the exact same way. Their fathers hurt them as little girls and then, as they grow up, men continue to disappoint their already wounded heart. When we as woman finally walk into the church and hear that God is our heavenly father the only reference we have is the hurt and disappointment from our fathers. Sadly, there is an epidemic of men who did not have fathers to teach them how to be men, in this nation. Men have made violence, self-gratification, manipulation and loud poor substitutes for quite gentle strength, courage, honor and integrity.

This decline in men being comfortable being real men has become, for many, the only reference we have of who God the father is. A life time of fears are projected onto God and the only assumption many of us can make as we are introduced to God the father is that he will do the same things.

It took me approximately nine years of attending church before I truly understood that there was a huge difference between my earthly father and God the father. I had to not only know, for myself what his word says but even more I needed to know him, to observe his character and nature before I was able to risk trusting him. For me experiencing his personal love despite all of my flaws played a big role in my healing. And to all of my precious sisters reading this now he truly loves you as well flaws and all. I will say that you have to experience it for yourself you have to be willing to dig into God's word to trust God to pray to him to build the relationship with him in order to understand and truly grasp in your heart that he does love you and he wants the best for you. I'm not going to tell you that it's easy but I will tell you that it's worth it. God only wants the best for us. I know that there may even be some of you that has been hurt by either a pastor or a deacon in the church and you think that that is God and it is not. God is nothing like mortal man his love is unconditional.

GODS LOVE

1 John 4:8 - Whoever does not love does not know God, because God is love.

Romans 8:37-39 - No, in all these things we are more than conquerors through him who loved us. 38 For I am convinced that neither death nor life, neither angels nor demons,[a] neither the present nor the future, nor any powers, 39 neither height nor depth, nor anything else in all creation, will be able to separate us from the love of God that is in Christ Jesus our Lord.

John 3:16 - For God so loved the world that he gave his one and only Son, that whoever believes in him shall not perish but have eternal life.

Jeremiah 29:11 - For I know the plans I have for you," declares the Lord, "plans to prosper you and not to harm you, plans to give you hope and a future.

1 John 4:9-12 - This is how God showed his love among us: He sent his one and only Son into the world that we might live through him. 10 This is love: not that we loved God, but that he loved us and sent his Son as an atoning sacrifice for our sins. 11 Dear friends, since God so loved us, we also ought to love one another. 12 No one has ever seen God; but if we love one another, God lives in us and his love is made complete in us.

Romans 5:8 - But God demonstrates his own love for us in this: While we were still sinners, Christ died for us.

Psalm 36:5 - Your love, Lord, reaches to the heavens, your faithfulness to the skies.

Luke 12:7 - Indeed, the very hairs of your head are all numbered. Don't be afraid; you are worth more than many sparrows.

Psalm 103:11 - For as high as the heavens are above the earth, so great is his love for those who fear him;

Isaiah 49:15-16 - "Can a mother forget the baby at her breast and have no compassion on the child she has borne? Though she may forget, I will not forget you! 16 See, I have engraved you on the palms of my hands; your walls are ever before me.

Isaiah 54:10
Though the mountains be shaken and the hills be removed, yet my unfailing love for you will not be shaken nor my covenant of peace be removed," says the Lord, who has compassion on you.

GOD THE FATHER

1 Corinthians 8:6 - Yet for us there is but one God, the Father, from whom all things came and for whom we live; and there is but one Lord, Jesus Christ, through whom all things came and through whom we live.

Ephesians 4:6 - One God and Father of all, who is over all and through all and in all.

Matthew 23:9 - And do not call anyone on earth 'father,' for you have one Father, and he is in heaven.

Malachi 2:10 - Do we not all have one Father[a]? Did not one God create us? Why do we profane the covenant of our ancestors by being unfaithful to one another?

Psalm 68:5 - A father to the fatherless, a defender of widows, is God in his holy dwelling.

Isaiah 63:16 - But you are our Father, though Abraham does not know us or Israel acknowledge us; you, Lord, are our Father, our Redeemer from of old is your name.

James 1:17 - Every good and perfect gift is from above, coming down from the Father of the heavenly lights, who does not change like shifting shadows.

2 Corinthians 1:3-4 - Praise be to the God and Father of our Lord Jesus Christ, the Father of compassion and the God of all comfort, 4 who comforts us in all our troubles, so that we can comfort those in any trouble with the comfort we ourselves receive from God.

SELF-CHECK

What was your relationship with your father?

_____

_____

_____

_____

_____

_____

If it was unhealthy, why was it unhealthy?

_____

_____

_____

_____

_____

_____

_____

Do you struggle with God being your heavenly father? If so, why?

_____

_____

_____

_____

_____

_____

What can you do in order to build that trust with God and are you willing?

_____

_____

_____

_____

_____

_____

_____

Dreams are Born

December is the month of Jesus' birth we celebrate the ultimate dream which is our salvation. Can you imagine what our lives would be like? We would still be under the Old Testament law. But to us a savior was born! He came as flesh and his desire is that all of us would be saved! Jesus was born and died perfect yet he took on our sin and died a sinner's death. That was his entire purpose!

We are each born with dreams in our heart, he places them there. The bible says that God gives us the desires of our heart and what most people don't realize is that HE is the one that placed those desires in us!

My dream, passion, purpose and mission is to help women all over the world to heal from past hurts. I long to see women, who have been hurt and discarded, move forward into full and powerful lives. I love being able to motivate, inspire and empower women. That is the gift that God has given to me. For much of my life that dream was held captive by my shame. I refuse to allow my past secrets and scars to stop me from living out my purpose. It took a long time to realize that it's because of my scars and hurts that I can have compassion and hope to encourage others as they strive to overcome!! Who would have ever thought that me, a human trafficking survivor, abuse survivor, a woman that was filled with fear, guilt, shame, resentment and anger would now be a public speaker and an author, helping women all over the world? Turn that pain into your purpose! Don't rob someone that needs you of hearing your story! Be bold, be courageous and be great! Hold your head up high! You can do this! Don't allow what someone has done to you keep you from being all that you can be!

The following are definitions of dreams, goals, purpose, gifts & talents according to Webster's (Merriam-Webster Dictionary, n.d.)**dictionary:**

Dreams: an aspiration; goal; aim:

Goals: the result or achievement toward which effort is directed; aim; end

Purpose: the reason for which something exists or is done, made, used, etc.

Gifts: a special ability or capacity; natural endowment; talent

Talents: 1. a special natural ability or aptitude 2. a capacity for achievement or success; ability

Psalm 37:4 - Delight yourself in the Lord, and he will give you the desires of your heart.

Mark 11:24 - Therefore I tell you, whatever you ask in prayer, believe that you have received it, and it will be yours.

Matthew 6:33 - But seek first the kingdom of God and his righteousness, and all these things will be added to you.

Psalm 37:1-40 - Of David. Fret not yourself because of evildoers; be not envious of wrongdoers! For they will soon fade like the grass and wither like the green herb. Trust in the Lord, and do good; dwell in the land and befriend faithfulness. Delight yourself in the Lord, and he will give you the desires of your heart. Commit your way to the Lord; trust in him, and he will act.

Jeremiah 29:11 - For I know the plans I have for you, declares the Lord, plans for welfare and not for evil, to give you a future and a hope.

Proverbs 16:4 - The Lord has made everything for its purpose, even the wicked for the day of trouble.

Psalm 138:8 - The Lord will fulfill his purpose for me; your steadfast love, O Lord, endures forever. Do not forsake the work of your hands.

Ephesians 2:10 - For we are his workmanship, created in Christ Jesus for good works, which God prepared beforehand, that we should walk in them.

1 Peter 4:10 - As each has received a gift, use it to serve one another, as good stewards of God's varied grace.

Romans 11:29 - For the gifts and the calling of God are irrevocable.

Self-Check

What do you think your purpose is?

_____

_____

_____

_____

_____

_____

_____

Do you think you are walking in your purpose?

_____

_____

_____

_____

_____

_____

_____

What hindrances do you have in your life that could keep you from walking in your purpose?

_____

_____

_____

_____

_____

What goals do you have?

_____

_____

_____

_____

Where do you see yourself by this time next year?

_____

_____

_____

_____

_____

_____

Do you know the steps on how to get there?

_____

_____

_____

_____

_____

_____

_____

What is keeping you from achieving your goals?

_____

_____

_____

_____

_____

_____

_____

_____

What gifts do you possess?

_____

_____

_____

_____

_____

_____

_____

What do you plan to do with those gifts?

_____

_____

_____

_____

_____

_____

_____

What are your talents?

_____

_____

_____

_____

_____

_____

_____

How do you plan to use your talents?

_____

_____

_____

_____

_____

_____

_____

Walking It Out

All throughout the bible we hear God talk about obeying his commands. His Word is our guide on how to live everyday life but it's not always easy to follow. In Matthew 7:14 it says "For the gate is narrow and the way is hard that leads to life, and those who find it are few." BUT if we follow HIS guiding and his Word our lives can be more peaceful. We don't change overnight but if we take those baby steps we CAN and WILL change as well as heal from past/current hurts. ALL things are possible with God!!!!

Can you think of things in your life that cause you to stumble? Here are some examples: anger, the need for control, frustration, low self-esteem, worry, people pleasing, gossip, harsh tongue. The list can go on and on!!

Webster's (Merriam-Webster Dictionary, n.d.) **dictionary defines anger as:**
: a strong feeling of being upset or annoyed because of something wrong or bad: the feeling that makes someone want to hurt other people, to shout, etc.: the feeling of being angry.

Anger was a huge issue for me! I had bottled up so many things for so long that I was a ticking time bomb ready to explode at any given moment. If someone looked at me crazy I would go off on him or her. I would cuss them out and would literally be ready to fight! If I was to be totally honest, I had so much rage inside of me. It was much worse than anger. I would throw things; break things just to get the rage out. I needed a release. But breaking things, throwing things and punching walls was definitely NOT the answer. I had to get down to the core of my anger, which was the hurts and secrets I had kept inside for so long. This did not happen overnight. Keeping my temper under control has been some hard work. I had to learn not to let the "little" things bother me. As I started to heal my anger started to lessen. I have now become aware of what my triggers are and I can actually feel when I am getting to the point of rage. I feel it rising from the pit of my stomach and in that moment I work on breathing exercises or get somewhere quiet if possible and pray. Now I won't say I don't always get it right but I am far better than I used to be. Journaling has been another way that has helped with controlling my anger. I am able to write whatever is bothering me and get it out. You have to do what works for you. Going to the gym, running, kickboxing classes or some type of physical activity may help you get the release out. But no longer can we hold things in.

SELF-CHECK

Do you struggle with anger? If so, how?

_____

_____

_____

_____

_____

_____

What can you do to release your anger in a healthier way?

_____

_____

_____

_____

_____

_____

Psalm 37:8 Refrain from anger, and forsake wrath! Fret not yourself; it tends only to evil.

Proverbs 14:29 Whoever is slow to anger has great understanding, but he who has a hasty temper exalts folly.

James 1:19-20 Know this, my beloved brothers: let every person be quick to hear, slow to speak, slow to anger; For the anger of man does not produce the righteousness of God.

Ephesians 4:26-27 Be angry and do not sin; do not let the sun go down on your anger, and give no opportunity to the devil.

Proverbs 15:18 A hot-tempered man stirs up strife, but he who is slow to anger quiets contention.

Webster's (Merriam-Webster Dictionary, n.d.)**dictionary defines control as:**
: to direct the behavior of (a person or animal) : to cause (a person or animal) to do what you want : to have power over (something or someone) : to direct the actions or function of (something) : to cause (something) to act or function in a certain way.

Do you struggle with needing to be in control of everything? I know I have. For so many years' other people controlled me and everything about me that once I was free from their control I wasn't going to give up control to ANYBODY! That even included my husband and God!

What happened for me was that if things didn't go the way I planned them and I was losing control of the situation it would bring on my anger. I had to learn how to allow my husband to take control of some of the things in our household and include him in on decisions that I needed to make. I needed to learn to give control up to God and trust that HE would give me the wisdom when I needed to make decisions. Today, I don't have to be in control of everything. I have even found that I don't even want control of everything because that also brings a lot of stress.

SELF-CHECK

Do you find yourself having to control everything? Why?

_____

_____

_____

_____

_____

_____

Webster's (Merriam-Webster Dictionary, n.d.) **dictionary defines worry as:**

: to think about problems or fears: to feel or show fear and concern because you think that something bad has happened or could happen.

Proverbs 3:5 - Trust in the Lord with all your heart, and do not lean on your own understanding.

Philippians 4:6-7 - Do not be anxious about anything, but in everything by prayer and supplication with thanksgiving let your requests be made known to God. And the peace of God, which surpasses all understanding, will guard your hearts and your minds in Christ Jesus.

John 14:27 - Peace I leave with you; my peace I give to you. Not as the world gives do I give to you. Let not your hearts be troubled, neither let them be afraid.

Matthew 6:25-34 - "Therefore I tell you, do not be anxious about your life, what you will eat or what you will drink, nor about your body, what you will put on. Is not life more than food, and the body more than clothing? Look at the birds of the air: they neither sow nor reap nor gather into barns, and yet your heavenly Father feeds them. Are you not of more value than they? And which of you by being anxious can add a single hour to his span of life? And why are you anxious about clothing? Consider the lilies of the field, how they grow: they neither toil nor spin, yet I tell you, even Solomon in all his glory was not arrayed like one of these.

Worry was a huge thing for me! I constantly worried about how bills would be paid, how situations would turn out, what people were going to say about me, etc. My brain would never stop. I would even go as far as playing out a situation that hadn't even happened yet! It would drive me absolutely crazy! I would throw myself into an anxiety attack just because of worrying so much. But let me tell you what I have learned about worrying. Worrying about a situation won't change it. Instead of becoming all panicky about a situation, come up with a solution. Pray about it. Ask God to give you the wisdom you need and tell him your concerns and your needs. I have had to learn and am still learning that I need to go to God for all of my needs and trust that HE will provide for ALL of my needs. Not just some of them but all of them.

SELF-CHECK

Do you struggle with worry?

_____

_____

_____

_____

_____

_____

What are the things you worry about?

_____

_____

_____

_____

_____

_____

_____

What can you do differently?

_____

_____

_____

_____

_____

_____

Webster's (Merriam-Webster Dictionary, n.d.)**dictionary defines gossip as:**
: a person who often talks about the private details of other people's lives.

Ephesians 4:29 Let no corrupting talk come out of your mouths, but only such as is good for building up, as fits the occasion, that it may give grace to those who hear.

Proverbs 16:28 A dishonest man spreads strife, and a whisperer separates close friends.

Proverbs 11:13 Whoever goes about slandering reveals secrets, but he who is trustworthy in spirit keeps a thing covered.

Proverbs 6:16-19 There are six things that the Lord hates, seven that are an abomination to him: haughty eyes, a lying tongue, and hands that shed innocent blood, a heart that devises wicked plans, feet that make haste to run to evil, a false witness who breathes out lies, and one who sows discord among brothers.

Proverbs 20:19 Whoever goes about slandering reveals secrets; therefore, do not associate with a simple babbler.

Gossip was another area I struggled with. If someone did something to hurt my feelings I made sure everybody knew about it. It was usually because I didn't like the person so I would gossip and slander them in order to make myself look better. If someone was telling something "juicy" about somebody I wanted in on it. But as I grew and changed the one thing I learned about gossip is if somebody is talking to you about someone else you can best believe they are talking about you to someone else. I want to be a woman of integrity and I can't be if I am listening to gossip or talking about others in a hurtful way. It's just not worth it to me. My integrity and what God sees in me is much more important than what someone has to gossip about.

SELF-CHECK

Do you struggle in the area of gossip? _____

Why do you feel the need to gossip or listen to gossip?

_____

_____

_____

_____

_____

_____

What can you do differently to stop gossiping or listening to gossip?

_____

_____

_____

_____

_____

_____

Before we can change we have to be able to take a look at ourselves and admit that we struggle in certain areas. Change can only come if we do this in honesty!! Awareness is key to change. Once we know what we struggle with then we need to figure out what our "triggers" or signs are. An example of a sign for me when I know I am about to really blow up is I get a knot in my stomach, my face and ears got hot and my heart starts racing. Another example is when I want to be in control over a situation – it's as if an overwhelming obsession comes over me, it's all I can think about – I can't concentrate on anything else except how I can change a situation. I know when I start acting a certain way I need to immediately stop what I am doing, breath and step away from whatever it is. I may need to take a walk, do something to quite my mind or if I am at work I go in the bathroom and pray, even if it's only "Help me NOW Lord, I'm about to lose it". What ways can you think of to keep you from acting out from things that cause you to stumble? It is so important for us to become aware and then have a plan in place in order to not act out!!

God never wants us to stumble and he wants us to be able to go to him when we feel weak. He will strengthen us and guide us to WALK IT OUT!!!

Appendix: Citations & Resources

Works Cited

Got Questions Ministries. (n.d.). *What Does The Bible Say about Forgiving Yourself*. Retrieved from GotQuestions.org: https://www.gotquestions.org/forgiving-yourself.html
Merriam-Webster Dictionary. (n.d.). *www.merriam-webster.com*. Retrieved from Merriam-Webster.com: **https://www.merriam-webster.com**

If you suspect someone is being trafficked call 911. If you

want more information regarding human trafficking contact

National Human Trafficking Resource Center at:

Hotline: Call (888)373-7888

Or text HELP or INFO to BeFree (233733)

Hours: 24 hours, 7 days a week

Languages: English & Spanich

Website: traffickingresourcecenter.org

You can also learn more at www.polarisproject.org

About the Author

Kelley Alsobrook was born and raised in Miami, Florida and currently resides in Memphis, TN with her husband for the past 16 years. Kelley is a speaker, mentor, radio show host and advocate and survivor of human trafficking, domestic violence and sexual assault. She is now passionate about seeing those who have been beaten, broken, battered, and bruised become whole. This was the motivation for beginning Empower U. Kelley also started an Internet radio show called Empower U Radio in order to create a platform for human trafficking survivors to share their messages of hope.

Mrs. Alsobrook has earned her Associates Degree in Business Management and is currently pursuing her Bachelor's Degree in Criminal Justice. She has also become extremely involved in her community through speaking and educating those on human trafficking, as well as serving as an advocate in this same area.

She is an active member in her church, an active member of the Zeta Phi Beta Sorority, Inc. Amicae Auxiliary and has also served as president and vice president for The Voice of Raleigh Frasier, and was a board member on The Board of Walking Into a New Life.

Mrs. Alsobrook was the recipient of the 2011 S.I.S Award and received 1st place for her survivor story from Miracles House of Restoration in 2012 and was nominated for the

Shelby County Advocate of the Year award in 2013 as well as the Visionary Award in 2014.

Mrs. Alsobrook has been happily married to a wonderful man for the past 14 years. She has two daughters, one of which lives here in Memphis and has given her five beautiful grandchildren.

If you would like to learn more about EmpowerU and how you can help please visit their website at: www.kelleyalsobrook.com

Made in the USA
Charleston, SC
12 March 2017